THE GOOD DOCTOR

THE
GOOD
DOCTOR

BRINGING HEALING TO THE HOPELESS

BY SAI R. PARK, M.D.

Biblica Publishing
We welcome your questions and comments.

1820 Jet Stream Drive, Colorado Springs, CO 80921 USA
www.Biblica.com

The Good Doctor
ISBN-13: 978-1-60657-084-5

Published in 2010 by Biblica Publishing

A catalog record for this book is available through the Library of Congress.

Printed in the United States of America

Russia

China

Ussirisk clinic site

Najin–Sunbong

Shen Yang

Jian clinic site

Jang Baek clinic site

Dan Dong
Hospital

Sin Eu Ju

North Korea

Pyong Yang

Wonsan

Sariwon

DMZ(Demilitarized Zone)

Seoul

South Korea

Pusan

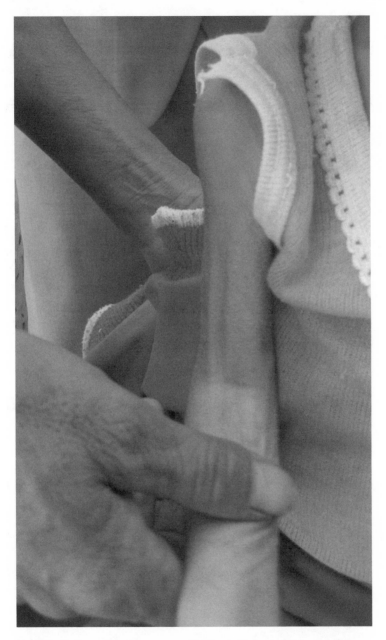

Severely malnourished two-year-old North Korean child treated by our medical team. At the time this photo was taken, she weighed only twelve pounds.

AUTHOR'S NOTE

A great deal has been heard about North Korea in the news recently regarding its controversial nuclear weapons proliferation and testing. But, in actuality, very little is known to the outside world about this strange, isolated country and the occurrences within, hidden and undetected from the world community for the better part of sixty years.

The world is slowly awakening to gripping details of an unprecedented famine that has devastated North Korea since the mid-1980s. Augmented relief efforts continue to be mobilized by international aid organizations, and yet, the famine still continues to rage on, unabated. People living in the most rural areas of the country are locked in desperate struggles for survival.

Controversy regarding the lack of transparency of distribution of international relief goods sent into the country lead many to wonder whether these life saving items truly reach the suffering people they are intended for. With borders drawn shut and exposure to the outside world reduced to a minimum, the North Korean government maintains its current power structure at all costs.

In this communist country no one is allowed in and no one is allowed out. North Korea considers this isolationism their independence from global persuasion and unnecessary external forces. There is no country on earth whose people's lives are more firmly ensconced in this ideology. And yet, if they are to survive, they will require ongoing and intensive aid from the international community. And if there is ever peace to be found among nations, North Korea is a country that needs the healing touch and divine saving grace of our Lord Jesus Christ.

SAI PARK, M.D.

Dr. Park is an OB/GYN and professor emeritus from the University of California-Davis Medical School. Dr. Park is also the Founder and President of Spiritual Awakening Mission Care, International (SAM-Care). SAM-Care is a non-profit organization that aims to provide medical care and humanitarian assistance to the most desolate regions around the globe. More importantly, SAM-Care aims to share the light and hope of the gospel of Jesus Christ in these dark and forsaken regions. Currently, SAM-Care runs charity hospitals and clinics along the border region between North Korea and China and deploys medical teams traveling into North Korea to treat the poor and the sick. SAM-Care has a membership of over fifteen thousand prayer partners worldwide. The website is www.samcare.org.

PREFACE

God Saves

My frequent trips into North Korea and to churches on both sides of the Pacific left little time for anything else. So when a cancer patient came to me for surgery, I was already booked on a Friday flight to Washington, D.C., to preach at a church revival service over the weekend. The patient was insistent that *I* perform her surgery. Given my tight calendar, I scheduled her operation for the Thursday before I left. The surgery would be very involved and difficult as the patient's disease was advanced and aggressively metastasizing. I consulted with the patient and her husband about possible risk factors. "It's a difficult surgery; there's always the chance that complications could occur," I informed them.

"That's why I chose to come to you," the patient stated confidently.

"As I've already mentioned, I'll be leaving on Friday for D.C. I'll perform the surgery and my colleagues will take good care of you during your recuperation until I get back." She and her husband both nodded their heads in complicit agreement.

The surgery turned out to be very complicated, much more than I had expected. It took over six hours to complete. While at home later that evening, my thoughts remained on my ailing patient.

At three in the morning, my phone rang.

"The patient is barely alive!" It was the hospital resident physician.

I rushed back to the hospital and performed an emergency surgery on the patient. This operation lasted for more than three hours. Afterward, I was convinced that nothing more could be medically done to save this patient; I felt certain that her death was imminent. I returned home to quickly shower and change clothes and then headed straight back to the hospital to check on her in the intensive care unit.

Hearing of her grave condition, extended family members began gathering outside her unit to hold a vigil. The patient's husband remained by her bedside, watching intently for signs of improvement in his comatose wife. I placed my hand lightly on his shoulder and beckoned him to follow me out to the hallway for a brief meeting. He nodded his head and quietly followed. His eyes were bloodshot with exhaustion.

"We've done all that we can for your wife up to this point. As you know, I'm leaving for D.C. My colleagues here will do their best to take good care of your wife until I get back," I stated assuredly.

His face immediately flushed a deep red hue and he became visibly distraught. "How can you go anywhere while your patient is dying?" His hands balled up into tight fists and his voice shook with disbelief.

"Didn't we already agree to this prior to the surgery?" I reminded him as calmly and evenly as I could manage.

"THAT WAS ON THE ASSUMPTION THAT THINGS WOULD GO WELL. YOUR PATIENT IS DYING! WHERE DO YOU THINK YOU'RE GOING WITHOUT FIRST SAVING HER!?" he screamed.

In an instant, every eye was fixed on us in a moment of stunned hush. Conflict welled up inside of me. Lord, I'm incapable of doing anything further for my dying patient. How can I tell these people that I'm going away to preach the gospel and lead a revival meeting?

Father, what am I supposed to do? Should I stay, even though there's nothing more I can do for her, or should I go on to D.C.?

I called the family members waiting in the hallway into the patient's room and asked them to join me in prayer for the dying woman. Ignoring the expressions of shock flitting across their faces, I carefully cradled the patient's frail hands in mine and prayed, "Dear Heavenly Father, this woman's precious life is in your hands. I now commit everything to you and your grace. . . ."

As I resolutely walked out of the room, heading for the airport, I could feel the family's hostile resentment and great disapproval boring into my back.

As my flight took off, my pager began to rattle softly. At first, I did not immediately recognize the callback number flashing on the small screen, when it suddenly dawned on me that the patient's husband must have been trying to reach me. I immediately assumed the worst. "Ah, the patient passed away," I whispered somberly to myself. This deadly disease robbed this young woman of her life much too soon. What pain and sorrow her family must be suffering.

Upon landing in D.C., I immediately called the patient's husband. I expected to hear his furious voice screaming through the phone, "HOW ARE YOU ABLE TO EVEN CALL YOURSELF A DOCTOR?!"

But I did not hear an angry voice. Instead, his jubilant voice came bustling through. "Dr. Park, my wife is breathing. Her pulse and blood pressure have normalized. She has come back to life! The God you prayed to has saved her!"

God Almighty, thank *you*!

Thank you!

To the best of my professional knowledge, this patient was dying. Medically speaking, her disease was so advanced and metastasized, there was nothing more that could have been done to save her.

Yet, she lived. And continues to live.

I had always thought that it was *my* intelligence, *my* skills acquired through intensive training, and *my* talent that saved people's lives. How foolish and egotistical I was.

After that day, I spent much time repenting of my sinful pride before the Lord. It has been well over fifteen years since that incident. Today the patient is alive and well, living a healthy and happy life with her family.

And this doctor lives with the undeniable certainty that it is not I but rather, *He*, who is truly the "Good Doctor."

1

The Beginning: Spiritual Revival

Michigan, mid-1970. My wife was waiting for me with a nice dinner as she usually did when I returned home after a full day's work at the hospital. She was dressed up to go somewhere, and I suspected that she was up to something—probably another spiritual revival meeting at a nearby church.

She hurried me along. "Please eat your dinner quickly, or we're going to be late."

"Whatever it is that you're planning, I don't want to go. I can't go," I stated flatly.

"Why not? Why wouldn't you want to go and be blessed by God's words?" she countered and added that the special speaker was an ex-hooligan-turned-pastor who had won fame after his conversion.

"Why don't you go alone? In fact, you should go live there and not come back!" I snapped. We rarely had big fights or arguments, but occasionally we got into these kinds of spats over church events.

When we had first started dating, one of the qualities I had appreciated most about her was her respectfulness in not trying to cram religion down my throat. Many girls I had known had relentlessly tried to drag me to church whenever they could. When I had wished to date some girls, their mothers had usually insisted on my going to church. I had very little tolerance for God or formalized religion of any kind. My wife was not like that. She was very respectful, considerate, and I felt comfortable with her.

She had been a church pianist in South Korea, and with so many worship services, her life seemed to revolve around the church. In addition to Sundays, she was there throughout the week—Wednesday evening service, Friday night prayer service, Saturday morning service. I had not known that so many church services existed in addition to those on Sundays. On weekends, especially, I wanted to go to the movies with her or do something fun, but there was never any time. I became an accustomed lone figure, sitting in the back pews of the sanctuary almost every day, anxiously waiting for the services to end.

At that time, I put up with all of her church activities as I appreciated her trust in me and her efforts to accommodate my wishes as best she could. I did not tell her, but I figured once we were married and left for America, her life as a church pianist and her church days would be over forever.

After we were married, however, I discovered that she would wake up at four o'clock *every* morning to pray, usually in another room. Although I hinted at my great disapproval of this annoying habit, she would not budge on this particular issue. One morning I happened to overhear her praying, "Please lead my husband to thirst for you, Lord, and to live a life full of your grace."

"No matter how hard you pray," I told her smugly, "don't expect me to change."

I was wrong to assume that coming to America would mean an end to our church life. When we first arrived in Baltimore in 1966, there were very few Koreans living in the U.S. We began holding worship services with just five other Korean families at our home, as a pioneering effort. Soon, a church was found to hold the services, and going to church on Sundays became an established routine. I begrudgingly went along, feigning interest as I muttered futile complaints under my breath.

Many guest pastors visited, and my wife began arranging small meetings and services at our home. I usually joined them, understanding the welcome relief and camaraderie church activities provided as an alleviation from the intense loneliness experienced by many immigrants in a foreign land.

In addition to the Sunday services, I even tolerated the special revival meetings held at our church. However, the problem was that my wife also wanted to take me to revival meetings held at *other* churches, which I literally could not stand. After all, it was out of "the sheer generosity of my heart" that I even attended the special revival meetings at our own church, to begin with.

So on that particular evening in the mid-70s, she was trying to do exactly that—drag me to a revival meeting at some other church. I stubbornly resisted and stated that I would not go. She was being equally stubborn and would not back down. Our banter became progressively heated, and soon her large eyes began filling with tears.

That was it! It was time for me to lay down the law. I drove us to a shopping center parking lot, as we did not want to quarrel in front of the children.

I grumbled loudly as I drove, "Why did I marry such a stubborn Christian? If I hadn't been so poor when I was a doctor in the Korean army and hadn't had to look for side work, . . . if only your father had turned me down when I had asked him for a job, . . . then I wouldn't have met my church-fanatic wife!"

After graduation from medical school, I had worked briefly for her father, Dr. Hwang, a pediatrician. He owned a small children's hospital in Pusan. One day he asked me to accompany him to church. I was very reluctant to go but followed along out of gratitude for the job he had given me. This was the first time I had sat through a full church service, and I wanted to make sure it was my last!

After that Sunday, I excused myself from attending Sunday services with him by stating my obligation to travel to Seoul every Sunday to visit my family. I went so far as to write a letter of apology for not being able to go to church with him. Ironically, it was that letter that convinced him that I was "a very sincere and good person," and that was how he came to invite me to dinner at his home one evening. There I met his eldest daughter. I think I just fell helplessly in love the first moment I saw her. There was something very special about her.

I parked my car in the parking lot.

"DIDN'T I TELL YOU THAT I WOULDN'T GO?" I screamed.

My yelling was no use, however.

She wept. She won.

It was that simple.

I ended up going to the church revival with my wife in tears. "This is the last time!" I warned hotly. "Don't even think of having pastors come to our house ever again!" I really put my foot down.

Firmly.

For me, having revival speakers or pastors at our home was more unbearable than the revival meetings themselves. I would always complain to my wife, "Please don't invite them over. It's just too much trouble."

"My dear, please meet with these good pastors and let them bless you." She had a very strong will. There was no budging her, not even a bit.

So I dragged my feet to the revival service that evening, upset and angry. A cacophony of bitter thoughts raced through my mind as I sat in the very back pew. I tried to listen intently to the pastor, wanting to catch mistakes in his sermon. I was determined to find an excuse so that she would *never* be able to force me to come to these church revivals again!

However, as I sat listening to this particular speaker, something completely unexpected occurred. I began thinking about what a wretched man I was. Ungrateful jerk, picking fights with your wife and yelling at her for no reason. Hot tears began filling my eyes as

I scolded myself, "You really are so arrogant . . . so smug . . . the stupidest of them all."

The End of Arrogance

For quite a while, I had been feeling suffocated by my life. The career, the fabulous home, the prestigious country club membership, the beautiful family, the wonderful friends, the extravagant parties, the golfing weekends . . . I had worked so diligently in the creation of all of this, and now I was being smothered by it all. My phones rang constantly, and I shirked in answering them. I wanted to break them into pieces. People might have envied my job—as an obstetrician/gynecologist—in which I was surrounded by women all day long, but I was getting more and more tired of it all.

After working with women all day long and arriving home exhausted—usually not before nine or ten at night—I did not want to see or talk to another female, not even my wife.

"I don't feel like talking to any female," I would tell her bluntly.

Because of my fatigued state of mind, my body also began to suffer: back aches, leg aches, headaches . . . I ordered medications liberally for myself from the hospital pharmacy, as if prescribing them for my wife. "Your wife is in such poor health. She seems to be a clinical case for every department of a general hospital," the pharmacy staff would often comment to me.

I also lashed out at my wife.

Frequently.

Although she often spent hours painstakingly preparing delicious meals such as my favorite daikon radish soup, I always complained, even as I enjoyed it:

"It's so salty!"

"It's so tasteless!"

Both my wife and children would tell me that I would be of more help if I just kept quiet.

Sometimes when I was very late in coming home, my wife would wait for me outside by the curb of our driveway. While I would feel simultaneously sorry and grateful at the sight of my wife waiting anxiously for me, my agitation and grumpiness tended to jump out at her first.

"What kept you so long? I had to warm your food several times."

"Did I tell you to wait outside? Just wait inside!" I would bark.

Her eyes would fill with tears. I felt so sorry, on the one hand, for treating my good wife so unfairly; but, on the other hand, I was just too exhausted to coddle her or anyone else. In fact, it took every ounce of energy I possessed, just to pull myself through the seemingly bone-crushing pressures of each day.

That evening at the revival, I realized that both my mind and body had become weak and numb. Suddenly, a thought entered my mind: It's not because of me, but by God's grace that I am who I am today. Where that thought had come from, I had no idea.

Then, I recalled a vow I had made to God long, long ago as a young man.

The Vow

South Korea, 1955. Our small family store went bankrupt just prior to my graduation from high school. This halted any thought of further schooling. As I had graduated as the valedictorian of my high school class, it made sense for me to pursue a college career. However, with the family finances in shambles, it was well over a year after graduation before I began to even entertain thoughts about pursuing a college education.

Entrance into universities in South Korea is dependent on two key factors: academic achievement in high school and performances on each individual school's college entrance exams. When I informed my father of my intention to study for the Seoul National University

Entrance Exam, he was delighted. Though he had no means by which to do so, he offered to pay for my trolley tickets for the commute to and from the library every day. Getting back on track was difficult and more challenging than I had expected. However, I stuck to my goal with fierce determination. Each day I left for the library at the crack of dawn and came home late into the evening.

I walked from the *Guro Dong*—a remote rural village on the outskirts of Seoul, which we called home—to the central library in Seoul. This trek took more than several hours each way. My method of studying was rather simple: I voraciously memorized all the high school textbooks available to me. Studying in the library was too difficult a task as I was too hungry to sit still. I had no money and food was a rare commodity. If I was able to scrape up one small meal a day, that was considered a good day. More often than not, I went two or three days without eating. Reading and memorizing as I walked and moved around seemed to make it easier for me to ignore the incessant protestations of my starving stomach. I focused intently on the books as if drawing in nutritional sustenance from them.

Identical to the accelerated undergraduate / medical school combined programs here in the U.S. for high achieving high school students, medical schools in South Korea are also two years of undergraduate classes and four years of medical school curriculum. Students are admitted into medical school directly from high school, dependent on high achieving academic performances. Before applying for the college entrance exams, I visited one of my former high school instructors and informed him of my intent to apply to Seoul National University (SNU) Medical School, the top-ranked school in the nation. I boldly asked him for a letter of recommendation.

"No question, you were an excellent student, but you've been out of school for more than a year. Honestly, at this point, I think that Seoul National University will be too difficult and competitive for you to get into now. Why don't you apply to a less competitive school?" he suggested.

"I have to make it into Seoul National University. If I'm going to make anything of myself, it's going to depend on my acceptance to this school!" I began to plead desperately.

Feeling great sympathy for the poor and starving student slumped before him, he relented and wrote the letter of recommendation.

The temperature was well below freezing the morning of the Seoul National University Entrance Exams. My most salient memory is one of shivering violently throughout the course of the day, my stomach raw with hunger. Winter had descended heavily upon the Korean peninsula and ferociously cutting arctic winds whipped mercilessly about. As I walked quickly along a frozen sidewalk on my way to the exam site, I ran into a friend. Seeing that I had no winter coat, he generously lent me his to wear for the day. He also shared a portion of his breakfast and gave me money for the bus fare. What would I have done without his kindness?

A few weeks later, the test results were announced. I nervously made my way to the Seoul National University campus, heading first to the College of Arts and Sciences. The liberal arts school had been selected as a second choice on my application form, just as a backup option. I was not wholly confident of my chances of getting into the medical school.

My eyes searched eagerly for my name on the acceptance list. My name was nowhere to be found.

Panic began to rise within me as my mind began spinning. I didn't even make it into the liberal arts school! If I didn't get in there, there's no way I got into the medical school. Seoul National University Medical School accepts only top-ranked students from the top high schools. Besides, I stayed away for one full year after my high school graduation. What chance do I really have?

Before conceding total defeat, I had to check every test result. I trudged slowly toward the medical school with a sense of fear looming in my anxious mind. I was almost certain that I had failed.

As my leaden feet and weakened knees carried me toward the medical school complex, I screamed inside, "IF THERE TRULY IS A GOD SOMEWHERE, PLEASE HELP ME! IF YOU GRANT ME ADMISSION TO THE MEDICAL SCHOOL, I'LL BE A GOOD DOCTOR AND DEVOTE MY LIFE TO HELPING THE WEAK AND THE POOR JUST LIKE ME! PLEASE GIVE ME A CHANCE! PLEASE SAVE ME!" It was a short, desperate plea, probably too sloppy to be called a vow.

To my utter shock and amazement, there was my name, nestled among the admitted on the acceptance list.

"YAHOOO!" I shouted elatedly, punching my fist triumphantly into the air. This was unbelievable! I felt as if someone would come at any moment to strike my name off the list, declaring that there had been some sort of mistake. Yet, there was my name.

"Thank you, God! Thank you! I'll surely become a good doctor!" I promised over and over.

All thoughts about my vow had been forgotten until that evening of the revival meeting. Suddenly, I recalled my promise to God as I sat in the back of the sanctuary, listening intensely for mistakes in the pastor's sermon. Hot tears began spilling down my cheeks. All this time I've been pretending to be high and mighty, but I'm nothing but a greedy and selfish wretch. Maybe I do need you, God. Are you there? Will you help me?

God Spoke to Me through Angels

In retrospect, my life has been one big puzzle. A stranger once stated to me that I would grow up to become a successful doctor.

It was 1950. The Korean peninsula was being violently partitioned, brutally gripped in the throes of the Korean War. Our family fled the northern provinces, seeking refuge in the port city of Pusan in the southern region of the peninsula. My parents eventually opened a small shop selling dried seafood at the Pusan International Market.

I was a fifth grade elementary student and in the afternoons after school had let out, I would carry my infant brother to my mother so that she could nurse him. I would then stay to help her, and we walked home together after closing the shop at night.

One day, an elderly man walked into the store and nonchalantly glanced in my direction as he passed by. Suddenly, he stopped in his tracks, whipped his head around, and narrowed his eyes as he stared at me intensely. "How old are you?" he asked.

"Ten," I responded, a bit puzzled.

"Where is your father?"

I pointed to my father in the distance. The gentleman marched stoutly up to my father and announced, "Congratulations on your son. He'll someday become a very successful and respected doctor and enjoy great honor and wealth in his life." Without another word, this strange man turned around and left as quickly as he had entered.

My father stood there staring after him, motionlessly. I remember the pleased expression on his face. I remember feeling highly pleased myself.

After graduating from high school in Pusan, I gave up any notions of going on to college. Our family seafood store had gone bankrupt, and we were unable to pay off any of our mounting debts. We relocated quickly. Shelving any ambition for a higher education, I followed my family to Seoul.

Our family of seven lived crammed in a tiny, squalid, dank one-room basement apartment in the heart of the capital city. I began searching frantically for work, procurement of something—anything—to help my distressed family survive. From a random acquaintance, I learned of a possible job opening entailing laundry work at a U.S. Army base. This "friend" boasted of his connections and his ability to put in a good word for me. "No problem, the laundry job is yours. I promise," he assured me. Contrary to my best intentions, I vertiginously flung myself and all my hopes onto the random assurances and fleeting arrangements of, basically, a stranger.

Each morning, I left home well before dawn and trudged one and a half hours through dark, expansive rice fields to reach the outskirts of Seoul. From there I took a thirty-minute trolley ride and walked another half hour before finally arriving at the U.S. base entrance. Day after day I waited. And waited. And waited. I expected someone to call me in at any moment, even skipping meals for fear of missing that person. Of course, I did not know the identity of who that person was supposed to be, but I just knew that the prearrangements had already been made. Someone was going to come and ask for me. They just had to. By the evenings, I would be famished and nearly in tears from exhaustion.

More than a month passed. I continued to wander aimlessly at the base entrance, waiting for a phantom opportunity to materialize, to no avail. I was ready to give up on the job. I was ready to give up on life. Why had I been born? Why was I alive? What a meaningless existence I had. I could not even get a job doing laundry!

"I have nothing," I moaned dejectedly to myself as I made the long, exhausting trek home one night. "My life is useless; there's no place where I can go and have even one decent meal." Deep despair consumed my heart as I stood there alone in the dark rice fields. I began to cry with howling abandon, exhaling my great sorrow and bitter disappointment into the dark, starless sky. There's nothing for me except death! Let me just give up now!

It was Christmas Eve. Mounting despair had confiscated any remnants of hope, and crushed me into a dark depression. I had fallen into an uncomfortable sleep, crouched in a corner with my head hunched awkwardly over my knees. I do not know how long I was asleep, but soft sounds woke me.

Silent night, holy night
All is calm, all is bright
Round yon Virgin Mother and Child
Holy Infant so tender and mild

Sleep in heavenly peace
Sleep in heavenly peace

Carolers were singing the hymn outside our dark basement, single-room window. Hot, anguished tears began burning my eyes. "How lucky are they! How pitiful am I! How did I end up living such a wasted, dreary existence?" I whispered to myself as I began to sob. The choir sang another hymn.

It came upon the midnight clear
That glorious song of old
From angels bending near the earth
To touch their harps of gold
"Peace on the earth, goodwill to men
from heaven's all gracious King"
The world in solemn stillness lay
To hear the angels sing

As I heard the second hymn, I forced myself to sit up. I can't die like this. I can't give up on my life. I want to live. I WANT TO LIVE!

I thought about what I did best. In what did I excel? What could I do? The only answer that came to mind was my ability to study. "Forget about finding a job at the U.S. Army base. Instead, I'll study. Yes! I'll go back to school, and not just any school, the top school in the country. I'm going to get into Seoul National University Medical School!" I said to myself defiantly.

To this day, the identity of those carolers remains a mystery, and I do not know how they came to be positioned exactly outside our apartment window. However, of this I am sure: they must have been angels sent by God to lift me from the despairing ghetto that had become my soul and to reinvigorate life and hope into my heavy heart.

Were it not for those hymns that evening, I might have remained paralyzed in that dark, hopeless abyss forever.

I continued to sit in the back pew, my mind lost in the dizzying array of long lost memories of my youth. Suddenly, the pastor speaking at the revival announced, "Tonight, I'd like to stay in the home of the gentleman sitting in that farthest back corner."

He was pointing directly at me.

My wife, needless to say, was thrilled. That night, the pastor came to our home and sat up with us late into the evening. Sharing his astonishing personal testimony, he counseled us in the process and ended with prayer for each of us. The entire time, I felt edgy, restless, filled with a prescience that the progression of my life was about to be dramatically altered.

The Bible Study

I took a leap of faith and opened my heart. As they say, I let go and let God. I made the firm decision to accept Jesus as my Lord and Savior, fully committing my life to Christ. I began to understand the transcendent beauty of the love and grace of our Lord. His precious blood had been spilled for *me* on the cross of Calvary, and His ultimate forgiveness of my multitude of sins cleansed away the vestiges of my former tortured, distressed self. I had new and meaningful purpose in this life and the next. The Lord's answers to my wife's prayers were finally being realized. She was overjoyed, to say the least.

Making this conscious decision to accept and embrace Christ fully resulted in surprising changes which pervaded every aspect of my life. Attending church was no longer a source of great irritation, the way it had been in the past. In fact, I began to look forward to it. Physical and mental exhaustion no longer plagued me, not even after coming home at midnight after a full day of service at church on Sundays, not even after a non-stop, frenzied day at the hospital surrounded by the endless pace of surgeries, patients, consultations, and hospital rounds. The world became a different place altogether. My environment had not changed; the people around me had not changed. Yet, *I* was different. A nascent shift was dramatically transforming my perspective on life and my purpose of being. Joy flooded my heart and soul and saturated everything—myself, the world, and my place in it. Even my wife's daikon radish soup never tasted better. With one spoonful of the soup, I felt as if I was partaking of a stupendous meal worthy of heaven's applause.

"Oh, Dear, it's so refreshing. How did you make it so good?"

"Don't mention it and just enjoy!" my wife would retort happily.

My physical ailments, the aches and pains that had plagued me relentlessly, vanished. I felt restored physically and renewed spiritually, no longer engaged in the deceptive facade of being a Christian in name only.

Not long afterward, the opportunity and honor of serving the church as a deacon—and then later as an elder—was offered. I did so with great joy and enthusiasm.

As our humble church began to quickly expand, the church deacons organized a Bible study that met an hour before the main Sunday worship service. For the first two weeks the study was led by our pastor, but due to his hectic Sunday agenda, he found it difficult to continue. I was asked to take his place. "Elder Park, would you consider leading the Bible study before the Sunday worship service? We'd like to have you teach the Bible for an hour."

I accepted the responsibility and picked up where our pastor had left off in his lessons on the book of Acts. With no seminary or theological training, I taught the Scriptures, inserting many of my own personal testimonies and experiences for emphasis. After finishing the book of Acts, my class and I began the study of the entire Bible, working our way judiciously from the book of Genesis through the book of Revelation.

My method of preparation entailed selecting several Bible verses to focus on for the following Sunday. Each waking moment was spent praying, pondering, reflecting, meditating, and concentrating on the verses in an effort to gain the Lord's wisdom. I did my best to put the Scriptures into practice and really make them my own. The Bible study hour attendance increased steadily in number, and the church began to distribute recordings of my teachings to congregants. An increasing number of people expressed appreciation for the tapes, stating particular enjoyment in listening to them while driving. Aware of the increased exposure, I often stayed up late into the evenings to prepare. I never missed a single Bible study hour. As I read, studied, prayed, and meditated on the Scriptures, the words began to capture and bless my soul. This was a period of great spiritual growth for me.

During my fourth year of conducting the Bible study hour, I began the formal study of theology to better equip myself with deeper understanding of God's Word. I pursued my theology studies with fevered intensity which melted away any desire for other potentially distracting activities—even golf, my favorite sport. When I did make time to play golf just to get some physical exercise, it wasn't as enjoyable. Other than time spent working in the hospital, nothing separated me from my full devotion to the study of the Bible.

Perhaps that was how God wanted to train me. Teaching the Bible study hour every week allowed me to gain a firmer understanding of His Word. I can confidently say that God provides us with the strength and capability to do the work in which He delights.

2

Longing for the Fatherland

They say that time lessens all wounds.

I was living life with a fresh sense of purpose and direction. There were no more grounds for silly quarrels with my wife. There was great joy in the realization that I was a child of God. And yet, I still harbored an unshakable sadness hidden deep inside.

After living a busy immigrant life for many years in the U.S., I found myself increasingly longing for my fatherland, the country from which I had run away, the country I had bitterly divested myself of, tossed away like a worthless old shoe. I was no longer filled with the intense antipathy I had had when I initially left South Korea. Time had dulled the razor sharp edges of the traumatic memories of my youth. I felt sparks of great joy when something good happened in South Korea and great pain when something bad happened there, as well.

During the 1988 Summer Olympics in Seoul, I cheered excitedly for the South Korean sports teams. Watching the games on television filled my eyes with nostalgic tears whenever the familiar tones of the Korean National Anthem were played and images of the South Korean flag billowed majestically across the screen. Perhaps this is akin to what Joseph felt upon meeting his brothers again, the same disdainful brothers who had once cruelly sold him into slavery in

Egypt. I felt glad that my fatherland had risen to join the ranks of the developed and prosperous nations of the world.

"Ah, I have a fatherland! I'm a Korean, too," I began to declare, adopting pride in my Korean heritage once again. At the time, I was being short-listed for the position of head of the gynecology department at the medical school where I taught. Being a department head entailed the management of a multimillion dollar budget as well as heightened prestige and esteem among medical colleagues. I coveted the position greatly.

Although I had graduated from a top-ranking medical school in South Korea, my dream of becoming a department head did not come to fruition—I suspect, mainly due to the fact that I had not graduated from a school with more name recognition here in the U.S. Although greatly disappointed, I held no grudges against the school administration for their decision. The experience, however, impacted me deeply. I began to think that perhaps returning to South Korea would be the best avenue to advance my career.

A university in Seoul was also aggressively pursuing me to head its medical school hospital. My wife and I made several trips to Seoul to follow up on the generous job offer. We grappled with the prospect of permanently moving back to South Korea. However, after having lived in the U.S. for more than thirty years, we had truly become Americans in the process. Additionally, South Korea had undergone an astonishing transformation in the time we had spent away. Technologically, industrially, culturally, intellectually, we no longer recognized the Korea of our youth. Curiously, my wife and I almost felt alienated there, as if we were foreigners in South Korea! In the end, we decided that we would not return. It did, however, instill in us a new appreciation and awe for the amazing country that South Korea had metamorphosed into.

With the soothing passage of time, memories and emotions that had once been dormant were being resuscitated, rushing back into being. I found myself dwelling more and more on my earlier days in Korea.

Seoul, 1963. Upon graduation from medical school, for three months I worked as an intern in a hospital surgical unit. During that time I witnessed the death of a man in his early forties; he died of complications from appendicitis. He had waited too long before seeking medical treatment because he had no money. I never forgot the experience.

Had he come to us for help just a little sooner, his life would not have been in jeopardy and his surgery would have been a simple routine procedure. Instead, he underwent a difficult operation and was moved to my unit to recover. I felt so sorry for this man and his poor circumstances. I stayed up several nights to care for him, even tending to him during my days off.

Despite our best efforts, he passed away on the third day. His family wept as they mourned his death, and I wept along with them. Poverty had claimed his life prematurely. He was a victim of his poor circumstances and had succumbed to a very treatable condition. This was my first negative experience as a doctor. The renowned doctors, for whom I had much respect and admiration, were powerless to save this man. Medicine had its limitations. Shouldn't all patients be cared for with the same love and respect regardless of wealth or status? Shouldn't all people have access to, at the very least, basic medical care?

My attitude regarding the type of doctor I wanted to be changed dramatically that day. I wanted to be humble about my life and profession. I wanted to be a medical advocate to help those who were too poor to help themselves.

However, any notions of these goodwill resolutions soon fell by the wayside after moving to the U.S. I was too engrossed in building my career, building wealth, and creating status. I was at the pinnacle of dazzling success and living the good life.

Little did I know that my attitude was about to change.

The Beginning of World Missions

Fall 1986. My wife and I organized a small prayer meeting for world missions. Once a week, church friends and medical colleagues joined us at our home for an evening of prayer and fellowship. We concentrated our focus on the lost, the poor, and the neglected masses around the world.

A few months afterward, I received a surprising phone call from my school. "Dr. Park, would you consider visiting three universities in India, including Bombay University as a visiting professor? Another American professor was supposed to go and now can't. Would you consider going in his stead?"

Bombay University Medical School had purchased the latest surgical laser machinery with the hope that an American professor would come to train their physicians regarding the latest gynecological surgical laser techniques and procedures.

"I'm not interested in going to India," I replied flatly.

"You may want to give it some thought. It could be a great opportunity for you professionally, not to mention the chance to travel to such an exotic country."

I told him no, but the idea stayed with me.

My wife believed it to be more than fleeting coincidence to be presented with an unexpected opportunity to travel to India, in light of the fact that we had started a prayer group for world missions. She asserted that it was God's mighty hand unlocking an entrance to world missions and that we should go together. I continued to pray, unable to dispel the intriguing notion in my head. When I finally made the decision to go, I decided that I would not only lecture at the medical schools but, during my time off, also conduct medical mission clinics in the countryside to serve the poor and needy. This was the first time in my life that I began to think about medicine in a mission capacity. My wife and I were determined to medically serve and teach the gospel while living among the locals.

December 1986. My wife and I left for India. We hauled heavy, overloaded luggage bulging full of medicines and medical supplies. The trip was a difficult endeavor from the start. It took two days to travel from Detroit to Bombay via New York, Seoul, Taiwan, and Bangkok. The plane to Bombay, in particular, reeked of strange, pungent odors so noxious, that I was nauseated throughout the entire flight. Sapped of strength and feeling half dead on the plane, I thought to myself, Going on a mission trip is not as easy as it had originally seemed.

We slipped easily through Indian customs, the officials barely giving our swollen suitcases a second glance. As we had determined before leaving the U.S., we did not stay in modern facility hotels with luxurious amenities, but instead at modest missionary guest houses.

I gave a series of lectures and surgical demonstrations at Bombay University Medical School. Afterward we left for Miraz, the location of India's most famous Christian hospital where I conducted a series of lectures and performed surgeries.

In Miraz, I met Dr. Archibald Fletcher, an American surgeon who had spent the bulk of his medical career in India, caring for patients as a medical missionary. I was fascinated by his uninhibited manner. He was well over seventy years old, but his energy and passion were boundless in caring for the filthy, rejected outcasts and unsavory members of Indian society. With openhearted generosity, he tended to each patient the way a loving father would look after his own children. In him, I found an extension of Christ—a gentle and caring Jesus. His endearing smile exuded unwavering enthusiasm for his work.

Observing Dr. Fletcher was an awakening experience for me. In living life as a medical missionary, Dr. Fletcher shared the importance of surrendering himself completely to the Lord's will and opening his heart and mind fully to the Holy Spirit's guidance. He stated that serving the Lord as a medical missionary was a calling from God. I began to really wonder whether God was calling me down such a path. Was I devoted enough, sensitive enough to His spirit, obedient enough to travel such a detoured life journey from the status quo? I also wondered whether I could truly follow Dr. Fletcher's selfless example of loving servitude all the way down into the dreariest trenches of Indian society.

Our final evening in Miraz, my wife and I stayed with Dr. Fletcher and his wife at their modest home. We shared a lovely dinner together and slept comfortably in their guest room, complete with plush Western-style beds. In the morning, we were immediately jolted awake, shocked by the sight of dozens of large, grotesque looking lizards crawling menacingly on the ceiling and walls. It was fortunate that we had not seen them before we fell asleep or we would have been too frightened to do so. We were thankful, at least, that while in Dr. Fletcher's home, we had not had to do battle with any scorpions, the way we had in the missionary guest houses.

Dr. Fletcher, now retired, resides in California. His wife recently passed away to be with the Lord after having walked with him for fifty-three years of missionary service. To this day, he remains as enthusiastic and passionate about Indian missions, as ever.

"But you will receive power when the Holy Spirit comes upon you; and you will be my witnesses in Jerusalem, and in all Judea and Samaria, and to the ends of the earth." (Acts 1:8)

The Scene of Poverty

My visiting professorship to India lasted three weeks. With the exception of a few days of lectures, surgical clinics, and demonstrations, my wife and I devoted the remainder of our time to treating patients in the Indian hinterlands. From Madras to Bombay we visited as many places as we could, treating up to three hundred patients a day. The American medicines we had brought with us were quickly depleted, and we replenished necessary medications by purchasing them locally. I drove myself hard to care for as many patients as possible, but was unable to physically keep up with my motivation and the demand. Exhaustion overtook me. Also, I was not emotionally prepared to face such destitute and deplorable conditions, the poverty-stricken faces, the decrepit bodies and souls. I was fearful of the swelling crowds of beggars that pressed in dangerously and flocked around us wherever we went.

I felt as if I had been transported back in time, standing helplessly in the middle of abject poverty again, the same poverty I had experienced in my youth.

Toward the end of World War II, as a child, I used to watch from an underground shelter as American bombers dropped thousands of bombs on Wonsan—a city in the northern province—at night. When daylight finally emerged, my family and I would crawl out of the shelter to find a grisly scene before us—mangled, bloodied, decapitated bodies and body parts strewn across the valley. Days and nights would continue like this. At the sound of an air raid warning, we would quickly grab food, blankets, and whatever else was within immediate reach of our fingertips and rush feverishly to take refuge in a safer area or an underground bunker.

I remember carrying supplies on my back and following my parents to remote areas away from the bombs. I did not know why the Americans were bombing our country and could not believe that I survived the bombings in one piece, day after day.

Then one night, the bombers completely decimated Wonsan. All night long, terrifying and brilliant flashes of light boomed and exploded, illuminating the black sky. Early the next morning, the Japanese emperor occupying the Korean peninsula quickly surrendered. The war had finally come to an end, or so we thought. Almost immediately, the Soviet army moved in, following our brief liberation from the hostile Japanese occupation. Our desperate hopes for peace splintered into utter chaos. Soviet soldiers broke into homes, looting and raping women every night. Women tried to flee to the underground shelters, but the nights still reverberated with the horrific screams of those being savagely raped and beaten.

The North Korean communists came after the Soviet soldiers. They hunted down and killed wealthy landowners and anyone who had collaborated with the Japanese. Friends turned into enemies and neighbors turned on each other. No one was to be trusted. It was a period of frenzied fear and panic. Those who survived the mayhem fled for their lives, and my family quickly headed for the southern provinces.

At our first attempt to escape, my family and I surreptitiously mingled ourselves in with a small group of people and managed to get onto a ship. We were soon caught by the Soviet soldiers and forced off. We attempted a second escape. This time my mother, my two younger sisters, and I hid in a small cargo vessel filled with dried fish. My father stayed behind to take care of unfinished business. Thus, my mother was left to lead us on this long, terrorizing escape by herself.

We eventually made it to Pohang, a southeastern city near Pusan. Life was anything but ordinary. There was no going to school. There was no going anywhere. We did nothing but anxiously wait for my father to reach us. Only after he arrived, did we move to Pusan, where my father's sister lived. But, life was dismal, desperate, wretched, and hungry.

Years later a triumphal moment would come for me and my family in the form of my acceptance into Seoul National University Medical School. My father beamed with pride. Despite my acceptance, we could not afford the registration fees, let alone the tuition.

Although SNU's fees were low in comparison to other private universities, my family could not afford to pay for anything. Regardless, my father told me not to worry. He would take care of it, he assured me. On the final day for registration of classes, my father miraculously placed enough money to cover the fees into my hands. At the time, I had no idea how he had managed to obtain such cash, but found out soon enough. It was not long before the creditors began harassing my father for payment. I knew then that he had borrowed the money.

When the creditors came, my father would respond: "I'm sorry but a pick-pocket stole the money on a bus. I have no way of repaying it now. Whether you kill me or not is totally up to you. However, if you save me, I'll work to my death to repay you."

His favorite phrase at the time was, "When my son becomes a successful doctor, I'll finally get to enjoy a leisurely trip around the country." I assumed that my father had borrowed the money from his fellow workers in the neighborhood market. Neither my father nor mother talked about it, and I pretended not to know. I knew that I was my father's best hope in life.

In my second year of college, my father suddenly passed away from tuberculosis. He took his last dying breath in the tiny, one-room shack we called home in the middle of the refugee's section of the city. Perhaps it was a relief for my father to abort his fleeting grip on life rather than be continually tethered to a futile and exhausting struggle to nowhere.

The temperature plummeted well below zero the day we buried him. As my family had no money for a proper burial, my friends from school kindly helped me to dig a small grave for my father's body. I gathered stray twigs scattered around in the snow and attempted to shape them into a respectable makeshift tombstone. As we buried him, waves of grief overpowered me and I sank to my knees heaving sobs of great sorrow and regret. It had been horrible to live with my father in the cramped one-room home. He depended on booze to comfort and anesthetize himself from the frustrations of his life. He had been raised without a father. His mother remarried while he was still little, but her new husband had no patience for children. Unwanted and unloved, my father was shoved off to be raised by an older sister, who became a reluctant surrogate parent by coercion. I used to hate my father's drunkenness and raucous diatribes that went on late into the night. His belligerent and deranged ranting and raving slashed away at my concentration while I tried to study, and there was nothing I could do about it. If I even dared to whisper a complaint, he would explode into a violent rage. "YOUR FATHER IS TALKING. HOW DARE YOU NOT LISTEN TO ME!" he would roar angrily.

If he ran out of alcohol at night, he would send me out to fetch more liquor from a neighborhood store, despite the military enforcement of a nationwide evening curfew. When sober, my father was quiet and demure and would gently encourage me to keep up with my studies. Under the influence of alcohol, he would become frighteningly uncontrollable, full of rage and fury. Both my mother and I were frequently and severely beaten by my father. Having seen what alcohol did to him, I made up my mind never to touch it.

Once while I was tutoring at a student's home, my mother came to seek my help. She was distraught. Her lips were swollen and bloody, her face full of angry bruises. My father had badly beaten her again. Enraged and furious, I ran home, ready to confront him, ready to beat him up. But when I saw the staggeringly drunk and incoherent state he was in, I burst into tears and turned back. How I had wished that he was gone! How often I had promised myself that I would never become a useless and abusive father like him.

Now he was gone.

He was dead, and I would never have the opportunity to hate him or love him anymore. I wept tears of overwhelming guilt and sorrow. "He could have lived a few more years if it wasn't for all the harassment and stress he got because of me . . ." He had borrowed money for my tuition and fees, knowing that he would never be able to repay any of it. I could only imagine the immense pressure he must have felt. It hurt to think that I had to send him away from this world without ever having had the opportunity to treat him to something nice—not even once. I hated my life and I hated that I no longer had a father. I was devastated beyond repair.

That day I strengthened my resolve to focus on nothing else but my studies. My grief and mourning propelled me to study with a singular-minded vengeance. I was determined to escape poverty and misery-stricken Korea. I was going to go to America and I would never come back.

So there I was in India, in the middle of wretched poverty, poverty from which I had struggled so desperately to escape. I felt as if we were treading through veritable trenches of miserable suffering and decay.

Riding an overnight Indian train was another ordeal. Owing to the scarcity of ethnic East Asians such as ourselves, people on the trains were endlessly fascinated by our presence. They openly gawked and pointed, staring as if we were caged monkeys in a zoo. Before sleeping, I would fasten my suitcases to my body with steel chains to prevent theft.

With no ability to communicate with the outside world, my wife and I became anxious about our children back home. We were physically and mentally spent and wanted nothing more than to return to the U.S. Thanks to Dr. Fletcher and his demonstration of perseverance, dedication, and heartfelt service, we managed to

Conducting medical missions in remote villages in the Indian countryside.

keep going until we had fully completed our medical missions in the Indian hinterlands.

Park Aya, Park Aya . . .

While conducting a medical mission clinic in Madras, an elderly woman came to see me, begging me to help her regain her failing eyesight. She had severe glaucoma, a condition that could only be corrected with surgery.

"You have glaucoma," I informed her. "You need to have surgery to correct the condition. You need to see an ophthalmologist at a hospital."

Since I was not an ophthalmologist, there was nothing more that I could do beyond diagnosing her condition. She continued to plead. "I'd have to wait three to four months to see a doctor here, and even if I do, they always give me the same powdered medication. It's useless. It hasn't helped at all, and now I'm almost blind."

I felt deep pity for the woman, but under the circumstances had no way of providing the specialized medical care she needed.

"I'm sorry, I don't have the means to really help you," I said apologetically.

"Park Aya (doctor), please save me. I'd rather die than become blind." She clutched my hands tightly as tears began streaming down her worn, craggy face. "Even if you don't have the necessary tools, please do *something* for my eyes. Use whatever you have. When will I ever see an American Aya like you again in my lifetime?"

I embraced her and began to pray. I asked the Lord to touch her with the miracle of His healing power and comforting grace. That was the best that I could do. I promised to bring an eye doctor with me the next time I visited.

"Park Aya, Park Aya . . ."

My heart ripped into two as I left, hearing her desperate, pleading cries call after me. How I had cursed my own poverty and struggled so fiercely to get out. Yet, people here were going through the same thing. The indigent members of society had no access to basic medical care. The need here was so great and the workers so few.

Life Is Worth Less Than a Stick

My wife and I visited the New Delhi Cremation Center. Corpses were burning in a facility the size of a football field. In the center, hundreds of cremation sites contained small blocks on which corpses burned in wood fires. The sickening, ghastly stench that arose from the burning corpses fouled the air all around. Unburned body parts lay scattered carelessly on the ground, due to the lack of firewood.

Many corpses were piled in a waiting heap. These bodies were not being treated with any more reverence or regard than the sticks that would be used to burn them. As a physician, I had seen many deaths and corpses throughout my career; but I had never seen anything this shocking. While corpses were burning, workers shoveled partially burned body parts into a river flowing next to the cremation center. I stood aghast at the horror of it all.

Down the river, a group of women crouched over the riverbed, fastidiously combing the muddy water with sieves. Curious, I made my way toward them. "What are you doing?" I asked one of the women.

"We're trying to find gold teeth or gold rings," she replied nonchalantly, concentrating intently on her sieve. I found the woman's casual reply and indifferent attitude more reprehensible than the repulsive stench and thick, oppressive smoke rising ghoulishly from the smoldering corpses.

This is life. Whether a person dies poor on the streets or immersed in splendor and luxury of wealth, when dead, each person becomes a corpse worth nothing more than a stick. If we human beings fail to clearly grasp from where we have come, our purpose on earth, and where we're eventually headed, we may not be any better than this in death.

I wanted to cry out to God, "Oh Lord, what should I do? What is the life that you really desire for me to live?"

Our short, three-week excursion to India proved to be a significant turning point in our lives.

A Taste of the Good Life

I used to think that I was smarter, better, and more talented than other people. Frankly speaking, I was probably more desperate. The single most predicating factor behind my unrelenting drive and compulsion to succeed was my intense desire to distance myself from any semblance to my days of hunger, poverty, and wretched misery. I pushed myself hard. Really hard. When our daughter Suzie turned six months old, I left South Korea for the U.S., after obtaining a position as an intern at Bon Secours Hospital in Baltimore, Maryland, a hospital affiliated with the Johns Hopkins Medical School Training Program. I came alone at first, and that was how my immigrant life began.

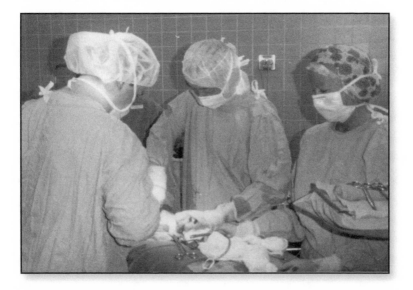

Performing surgery at Wayne State University Medical School Hospital.

I was lonely and terribly homesick in my new and unfamiliar environment with only a few Korean-speaking acquaintances around me. I missed my wife and daughter and found myself thinking of them often.

Six months later, my wife and Suzie joined me, and we settled down in a tiny apartment in Baltimore, Maryland. Due to my thirty-six-hour work shifts at the hospital, I was only given time to come home every other day. And when I did, I had no energy or motivation to interact well or meaningfully with either of them. I had become a stranger to my own daughter, as she would cry at the mere sight of me. My wife struggled to adjust to her new life in a foreign place and often broke down in lonely tears because I was too worn out to reassure her or to speak kind words to her. I would then complain about having no place to rest peacefully, either at work or at home. That was how we spent our days back then.

We lived with austere frugality. We had to. As a medical intern at that time, I was paid only $240 a month, after the deduction of taxes and airline ticket payments. Out of my monthly wages, $60 went toward the apartment rent, $60 for the car payment, $60 for my mother's living expenses in South Korea, and the remaining $60 for our living expenses. Despite the extremely tight budget, my wife never once complained about sending $60 to my mother each month. I cannot forget how immeasurably grateful I still am to her for that.

During the five years I spent as an intern and then as an OB/GYN resident, my wife and I had another daughter, Bette, and then soon afterward, a son, Terry. After my residency, I was given the opportunity to apply for a green card and did not hesitate at the first chance of becoming a permanent U.S. resident.

Upon finishing my training and fellowship, lucrative job offers and invitations from hospitals in South Korea began flowing in. They were not, however, in the least bit attractive to me. I was determined to never go back, as I had too many haunting memories of my poverty stricken youth.

In addition to spending four years of residency in obstetrics and gynecology, I spent another year specializing in female hormones and infertility. I continued my research and training in hormones and infertility as a research fellow at William Beaumont Hospital in Royal Oak, Michigan. As a result, I acquired specialist qualifications in two fields of gynecology.

After a year in a research fellowship, I accepted a partnership at a very successful medical team practice. At the time, I was also offered a teaching position at a nearby university, but declined the offer.

I wanted to make money—lots of it.

I worked at a frenzied pace, feeling that my efforts as an Asian American needed to be exponentially greater than that of my Caucasian counterparts. How else would a foreign doctor succeed in the U.S.? At the practice, I won the confidence of patient after patient. The number of patients under my care grew steadily as did my reputation as a competent and caring physician. Patients began lining up to seek my help, and I became extremely busy. I was an infertility specialist with microscopic surgical capabilities, and my medical colleagues referred many new patients to me. Some patients traveled from as far away as South Korea to see me. I also taught new endoscopy procedures to my fellow doctors, which eventually led to my appointment as the Director of Infertility and Hormones at our hospital and later to my position as a professor at Wayne State University Medical School.

As the number of patients continued to expand and my reputation as an infertility specialist solidified, I opened a practice of my own. With my own small hospital and a professorship at Wayne State University, I had nothing more in life to desire. Hospital OB/GYN departments are often as busy at night as they are during the daytime due to the obstetrics. I, however, was rarely bothered by middle of the night emergency calls, as I treated only infertility and hormone-related patients. I then bought the building in front of my hospital, which brought in a very good supplemental rental income.

I made a lot of money.

We marveled at the amount coming in. Each day, we would receive so many checks that we could not finish counting them all before the day's end. "Let's finish counting them tomorrow," we often said. Sometimes we became careless and accidentally threw checks away in the garbage.

We began to acquire many beautiful and luxurious things. We bought a gorgeous lakefront home built with an entire wall of panoramic windows overlooking a private golf course in an exclusive country club neighborhood. We even had our own golf cart and golf cart garage. My wife and I became avid golfers and often played on the neatly manicured greens of the picturesque golf course right in our very own backyard. We coasted along in an affluent lifestyle, enjoying all the splendors of extravagance and the best that money could buy.

They say that money buys happiness.

In an ironic twist, somehow, this statement did not hold true for me. Soon I found no satisfaction in having so many patients, and making a great deal of money began to feel unfulfilling, empty. I had finally gotten myself out of poverty and was living the "good life," but tormenting nightmares about the penurious days of my youth still haunted me. I would often wake from these night terrors, trembling, and having to forcibly remind myself that they were only dreams. I tried unsuccessfully to ignore them. The memories, however, continued to lurk menacingly in my consciousness, and I began to feel traumatized by them.

Prior to my trip to India, I did not know why I had suffered such miserable poverty in my youth and why I had struggled so hard to survive. Even though I had pulled myself out of my desperate circumstances, I was not at peace. I was led back to experience similar scenes of poverty in India, only to be reminded of the hopelessness of my youth all over again. I did not know the reasons.

But the Lord did.

He knew that without these reminders I would have been consumed by the seduction of an unending pursuit of more—more success, more wealth, more status. I would have wandered aimlessly, indulging single-mindedly in worldly things without any sense of what was right and eternal.

Thank you, Lord, for showing me the true value of life through my difficult childhood and allowing me to taste dizzying success, status, and wealth, just to show me how meaningless and empty they really are.

I'll live for you now.

The Letter without a Return Address

I began writing a weekly column for the American edition of the *Korea Times Newspaper*. My column was mostly a series of life reflections based on my experiences in India. I wrote about new goals and my desire to live as a "good doctor" and missionary.

Many people responded with enthusiasm: "Thank you for your fine column"; "I repented in tears after reading your column"; "What can we do to help those people?" In addition, people began sending in monetary donations indicated for Indian missions. It all happened so quickly that at the time I felt assured that the Lord was directing me toward missions in India.

"Dear Lord, how would you want us to use these generous offerings?" I asked during my prayers. The thought occurred to me to establish theological seminaries in India. I made arrangements for Pastor Singh, an Indian Christian pastor I had met in New Delhi, to come to the U.S. to establish connections with American churches to muster support for the school. We eventually raised the necessary funds to establish the seminary and seventeen students were admitted. The school provided for the education and livelihood of not only the students but immediate family members as well—over one hundred people in all. Pastor Singh worked tirelessly, and my wife and I were behind him all the way.

One evening as I retreated to my study to peruse that day's assortment of mail, I noticed a plain, nondescript, white envelope without a return address. It had a Tokyo postal stamp stuck to the corner. I opened it casually, thinking that it was nothing more than random mail. However, it was far from being random or ordinary.

It was a letter from North Korea!

"Your fatherland invites you and your wife for a visit."

We were startled. The year was 1988, and the world was embroiled in the Cold War. Diplomatic relations among South Korea, the U.S., and North Korea had frozen to a tenuous impasse. Although my wife and I had been praying for world missions, never in our wildest dreams did we imagine a scenario of such surreal proportions. We pondered the North Korean invitation carefully. Given the current international dissonance, would we be physically safe while there? What if we're mistakenly accused of being communists or North Korean collaborators upon our return? What about the children? "Shouldn't just one of us go? In case something bad happens, at least one of us would still be around to care for the children?"

We finally decided that only I would go. However, the risk of going alone seemed too great, so I extended an invitation to Dr. Hyun Shik Chang, a general surgeon and a close friend from medical school, to accompany me. Dr. Chang was a great man of faith, served as an elder in our church, and had also been an active participant in our weekly world missions prayer group. He accepted the offer without hesitation.

We held lofty notions in our minds, ambitious and grand expectations of participation in international scale healing—camaraderie between nations, gospelyzing the neglected North Korean population, bringing about peace between South Korea and North Korea through the Good News, and perhaps, even the eventual reunification of the Korean peninsula through the Lord's blessings!

It was later that I received an official explanation for the invitation: "We were impressed by your writings in your newspaper column. We have as many difficulties, if not more, as those found in India and have been looking for Korean-American doctors who could help us."

The Lord was paving the way and directing my steps. He must have led a high-ranking North Korean official to read my newspaper column and extend the invitation. The Lord had truly opened these doors.

Despite our excitement and enthusiasm, we could not dispel the lingering reticence that continued to plague us regarding the many unforeseeable factors of our trip: What if we're accused of being communists? What will happen to our families? However, we both felt very strongly that it *was* God's will for us to go, and we were willing to risk our lives to be obedient. We contacted the U.S. State Department and consulted with the South Korean Embassy in Washington, D.C., informing both offices of our impending trip. At that time, the State Department prohibited U.S. citizens from traveling to North Korea, but their response to us was very encouraging. The officials informed us that the U.S. had no diplomatic relations with North Korea and that once we crossed over into North Korean territory, they would be powerless to protect us. However, they would not stop us from going, given the good purpose for our visit and the acceptance of our own fate, should any difficulties arise. Considering the circumstances and terse political climate, Dr. Chang and I felt that the State Department response was a generous one.

On December 30, 1988, as people preoccupied themselves with festive year-end parties, family celebrations, and elaborate preparations for ushering in the New Year, Dr. Chang and I left for North Korea.

3

The Holiday Inn Hotel in Beijing

We stood in a long line of haggardly looking travelers waiting to pass through customs at the airport in Beijing when a scowling young man in a dark hat approached Elder Chang and whispered, "Are you Dr. Chang?"

Dr. Chang and I were startled. We had thought that the customs area was limited to airline passengers only. Was this man a North Korean agent? The idea made us both extremely nervous. He turned out to be a staff member from the North Korean Embassy in Beijing. We did not know that anyone from the embassy would be coming out to greet us. He seemed annoyed, at first, by the delayed arrival of our flight and became downright irascible when he learned of our arrangements already made with a Korean-Chinese guide to help us navigate around China. He left in an agitated huff.

We stayed at the Holiday Inn Hotel in Beijing, where we would be able to communicate in English with the hotel staff and enjoy modern, Western-style amenities. The glass entrance doors gave way to a lobby that was expansive and beautifully decorated, adorned with rich and contemporary furniture and abstract art prominently displayed on the walls. The sleek, black marble floors had been expertly polished to a high gloss finish. The beautiful tones of Mozart floated melodiously from a violinist playing softly in the corner. Impressive. This was not something we had expected to see in China.

Still, feeling restless and anxious about our impending trip into North Korea, our prayers together helped us to eventually fall asleep.

Early the next morning, we made our way to the North Korean Embassy to obtain North Korean visas, only to be informed that the embassy was closed until January 3. Dr. Chang and I could not wait until January 3. Given our tight schedules, we would be forced to return to the U.S. if we were not granted entrance into North Korea promptly. We asked to speak to the consulate general, hoping that he would be able to offer some assistance.

As we waited outside the embassy's security guard office, Dr. Chang and I whispered prayers under our breath. An elderly man waited beside us, watching us with great curiosity. Suddenly, he exclaimed, "You must be Christians!"

"Shh! Keep your voice down! We don't want any trouble," I whispered tensely, quickly glancing around to see if anyone was hovering nearby.

The old man chuckled. "It's O.K. I don't think anybody would take us in. I'm "Y" Choi. I'm a Korean-Chinese from Harbin, and I'm a Christian too. I was a soldier in the liberation army. I heard that Pastor "S" would be coming to visit Beijing, and I came here to find out his itinerary," he stated breathlessly. His crinkled, weather-worn face cracked into an impish grin. We were astonished to learn that this elderly looking fellow was only a few years older than we. He was fifty-five and looked at least eighty. His breathing was heavy and labored despite the oxygen tank he used due to his hardening lungs.

Were unseen eyes and ears privy to this conversation? The risk was too great to continue our dialogue with Mr. Choi there. Instead, we arranged to meet him later in the evening at a cheaper hotel in Beijing, one that came *highly* recommended by Mr. Choi.

We waited for several more hours outside the embassy before finally being granted an audience with the consulate general. We explained our predicament. He informed us that he would have to check with government officials in Pyong Yang and instructed us to return the next morning. We left his office and, following Mr. Choi's highly endorsed recommendation, immediately checked ourselves out of the Holiday Inn Hotel and into the cheaper hotel.

That evening we met Mr. Choi in our cramped hotel room and heard many fascinating stories about the underground Christians in China and North Korea. He stated that there were many underground believers in Harbin—a northeastern city on the periphery of the North Korean border—but that many had difficulty in understanding the Bible due to a lack of reference books. Since no Christian books were permitted into China from the outside, Dr. Chang and I decided upon our return to the U.S. that we would unbind a Bible reference book and send it to the Harbin Christians in many separate envelopes, each containing a few pages of the book mailed under different names. The Harbin Christians could then collect the separate pages and rebind them into its original book form.

Mr. Choi also talked about North Korea in an uninhibited manner. "The Mr. Kim must die in order for reunification of the two Koreas to occur!" he stated boldly.

The phone rang shrilly and it made us all jump.

It was Pastor "L," a friend of mine from the U.S. who had been working in Beijing to assist people with disabilities and handicaps.

"Dr. Park, you've got to get out of that hotel as quickly as you can. It's dangerous to stay there. North Korean agents eavesdrop on every room in that building!" he warned urgently.

Alarmed, we immediately checked out of the cheaper hotel and moved back into the Holiday Inn Hotel.

The next morning, we returned to the North Korean Embassy as we had been instructed. Had someone heard our conversation from the night before? Dr. Chang and I paced the hallway nervously as we waited. However, the consulate general greeted us with a big cheery smile. "The fatherland has arranged a special flight for you," he stated brightly.

Dr. Chang and I were the only passengers aboard a North Korean chartered plane called the Chosun People's Airline. As we climbed the steps to board the aircraft, we noticed its tires were completely bald and wondered about the safety of the plane. Would this antiquated and battered looking machine be able to fly? Would it be able to land?

The flight into Pyong, North Korea, took a little over one hour and thirty minutes. Landing at the Pyong Yang Sunan Airport, we soon realized that the runway surface was so bumpy and broken that it would have stopped any plane, even one without proper landing gear or adequate tires.

I felt as if I was dreaming as I stepped onto the ground and looked around. It was January 2, 1989. God had called and led me there to save my fellow Koreans, their lives and souls! The Lord of grace had put up with me, walked with me, and embraced me in His love. He had ordered my steps!

At the same time, I was a little leery and wondered, "Why an unworthy person like me?" I did not know for sure, but I sensed a sweeping undercurrent of the Lord's will moving in exact accordance to His ultimate plan.

Tour of the "Battlefields"

"Welcome. You look much younger in person than you do in pictures," a North Korean official said to me as he greeted us in his thick Pyong Yang dialect, his piercing eyes darting around busily. I was not sure if he was making fun of me or complimenting me.

We were ushered into a private car and taken to our hotel. Grand buildings and sleek edifices looked grey in the chill of the winter sky, and many were donned with massive, red propaganda slogans. The most striking were those hanging in the Red Square:

"LONG LIVE OUR GREAT LEADER KIM IL SUNG AND THE KOREAN PEOPLE'S DEMOCRATIC REPUBLIC!"

"THE PARTY DECIDES; WE EXECUTE!"

"LET US FOLLOW THE GREAT LEADER KIM IL SUNG AND COMPLETE THE REVOLUTION!"

The red slogans hanging atop these buildings were intimidating, and the forceful expressions of their hardened resolutions and their repressive aim for the society made me feel very sad for the people.

We stayed at the Koryo Hotel, the most modern and most costly of all the foreigner hotels in Pyong Yang. Meals at the hotel restaurants were grotesquely elaborate and excessively laid out, multi-course feasts of which we had no other option but to partake. At first, other than time spent at meals, virtually every waking moment was spent listening to an unending barrage of mandatory lectures hounding, expounding, and extolling the virtues of *Juche*, the strange North Korean philosophical ideology of self-reliance. The North Korean officials insisted that if we were to help the fatherland, we would first need to familiarize ourselves with *their* ideologies and *their* ways.

After two full days of this, with our tolerance quickly dissipating, Dr. Chang and I voiced our opposition. As an alternative, they insisted that we embark on a sightseeing tour to observe the grandeur of North Korea. They offered first to take us to the Geumgang Mountains. We declined.

They then insisted that we go and at least survey the beautiful sights of the Myohang Mountains, closer to Pyong Yang. We again declined.

We had come to North Korea to fulfill the Lord's will to help the people and were unwilling to engage in frivolous, protracted games of procrastination by touring, sightseeing, or being forcibly indoctrinated. We informed them of our wish to see the hospitals, as we had come to offer medical help. Perhaps our grave and no nonsense attitudes helped us to win their confidence. One of the officials later said to me, "You must really love the fatherland. You're different from the others who've come here. So far, three thousand Korean Americans have been granted entrance to pursue long lost family reunions, but when they return to America, most usually do not keep their promises to help. It would have been better if they hadn't promised or hadn't come at all."

With permission coming through from higher officials to tour the hospitals, we followed our government guides to the most modern facilities in the capital: the Pyong Yang Medical School Hospital, the Pyong Yang Obstetrical Hospital, and the Kim Man-Yu Hospital. As we surveyed the run-down and deteriorated conditions of these hospitals, a more lucid understanding came over me as to why the Lord had sent us there. None of these facilities remotely resembled a hospital. Owing to a notoriously deficient supply of electricity throughout the entire country, the buildings resembled ice boxes, as patients waited silently in bone chillingly cold and darkened hallways.

The most shocking reality of all was the lack of basic and essential medical instruments and equipment. We witnessed a surgery of the removal of a cancerous ovary in a patient. Unbelievably, the North Korean surgeons had only *six* tools available for use in this operation, with the scissors and pincers completely dull and worn out. By comparison, in the U.S., surgeons have at their disposal over two to three hundred different surgical tools for use in even the most minor outpatient procedures.

There were no medications in any of the hospitals. The North Korean doctors we met, pleaded with us to send them *any* medicine, even aspirin and penicillin, upon our return home.

Also striking were the befuddling "Battlefield" slogans which were boldly displayed on every hospital ward:

"SURGICAL BATTLEFIELD"

"PHARMACEUTICAL BATTLEFIELD"

"NURSING BATTLEFIELD"

"Why do you call hospitals battlefields?" I asked one of the officials. "It sounds as if you're preparing for a war."

"We do that to encourage people to work as hard as they can, as if they were in a war situation," he responded gravely.

I could see the extent to which the whole society had become militarized. They worked and lived under harsh and deficient conditions, perhaps akin to those found during a war; but to call life-saving institutions battlefields was completely beyond my comprehension.

From the outside the Pyong Yang Obstetrical Hospital was a large, beautiful structure. Its magnificent exterior belied the forlorn sparseness of its interior. There were no medications, medical supplies, or equipment. Interestingly, nor did I see any pregnant women anywhere.

Our guides also showed us the Kim Man-Yu Hospital. They informed us that a wealthy Korean-Japanese man had donated the facility. The beds and medical equipment—all of Japanese origin—were modern and up to date. The conditions in this hospital were more advanced, and it served only high-ranking government officials.

As we made our way back to our car, a thought occurred to me, What if we were able to set up a hospital here, ourselves. We would be able to personally help and interact directly with the North Korean patients.

We were permitted to survey the Pyong Yang Grand Central Library. Rows and rows of shelves displayed thousands of neatly arranged tomes. Yet, we found none that were published after 1950. We could only conclude that from the time North Korea became a sovereign nation in the 1950s, communication from the outside world had completely shut down. The people's only sources of information were filtered through the government. North Korean television was fixed to two or three channels, with every single program dedicated to the praise and glorification of the "Great Leader." That was it. There were no competing or alternative sources of information permitted.

I was reminded of an expression that is often heard in South Korea regarding North Korean sentiment toward the South: "In South Korea, rich folks die of gluttony, and the poor die of starvation. Its women have become sexual playthings to the Americans. Reunification of the two Koreas must occur quickly in order to save the South Koreans."

Their hospitals had no medicine and their people had no food. The North Koreans were unable to save themselves. It was most urgent that we save them from their own pitiful demise.

Building Bridges of Love

"We built these facilities to co-host the 1988 Summer Olympics with the South Koreans, but they were completely uncooperative in the matter," our government guide stated as he pointed to several monumentally huge gymnasiums situated in a newer community in Pyong Yang. The gargantuan buildings stood virtually empty with the exception of a few national athletes there to practice. I shook my head in disbelief. I wanted to shout, "What good does it do to build such impressive buildings when your own citizens are dying from starvation and disease?"

The following morning we were taken to Mankyungdae, the birthplace of President Kim Il Sung. A young female tour guide dressed in a brightly colored traditional Korean garment (*hanbok*) greeted us.

"We welcome you to our fatherland. Mankyungdae is the birth-place of our Great Leader Kim Il Sung . . ." She seemed to have memorized the entire history.

"Our Great Leader has much love for the women of the fatherland. He allows us now to wear lipstick on our lips," the guide spoke proudly, her voice and intonation saturated with worshipful reverence.

They were allowed to use lipsticks only *recently*. I felt as if I had exited reality and jumped into the Twilight Zone. Women around the world would never believe this. This was yet another example of the extent of North Korea's extreme isolationism from the world community. If the borders ever opened up, would North Korean women still be content with only the ability to wear lipstick, especially after observing the stylish, expressive flair and fashion of cosmopolitan women around the world? Surely not. Once initiated, the unfolding sequence of freedom could never be stopped by any human force.

Our brief stay in North Korea provided a jarring glimpse into the government's indoctrinating ideals, firmly imposed upon the people, inextricably intertwined into every aspect of their everyday lives and culture. They existed in a grotesquely distorted unreality, one that was rooted in the unchallenged belief that acceptance of their harsh lives was a sacrifice necessary to achieve the ultimate goal of "destroying the enemies of the North Korean state" and "triumphantly completing their revolution."

To traverse the obstructing barriers of clashing political, cultural, and incongruous ideological differences, we were going to have to build bridges of love. And quickly. One half of our Korean people were desperately struggling to survive.

We Don't Need God; We Have Our Great Leader

The first Sunday of January 1989, Dr. Chang and I attended a worship service at the Bongsu Church in Pyong Yang. The church had been constructed just a year earlier and the interior remained unfinished. The building had no heat, and the air inside was as frosty as it was outside. A colorfully ornamented Christmas tree stood in the corner, and the dull gray concrete floors exuded a somewhat eerie ambience.

No matter.

Elder Chang and I were absolutely *elated* to be singing hymns and praying openly to the Lord, right there in the heart of North Korea! Despite the frigid temperature, about two hundred people were in attendance. Oddly enough, every woman was dressed in identical coordinated outfits of white tops and black skirts, almost as if wearing uniforms. There was no organ or choir. The pastor began his sermon on the book of Luke: "We must turn this world into a heaven. This is what the communist revolution is all about. We're trying to build the best socialist country here in North Korea. Let's pray for the continuation and success of socialism according to our Great Leader's will."

What began as a teaching from the book of Luke ended with praise for the "Great Leader." After the service the entire congregation gathered outside to greet us. The congregants were cordial and we took pictures with many, including both the principal and the associate pastors. That particular Sunday, the Bongsu church became the most beautiful place of worship on earth and through our participation in that morning's service, Dr. Chang and I felt enormously blessed, surrounded by His majestic grace.

"Of course there's freedom of religion in our fatherland. Those who want to worship at home can worship at home. Those who want to go to church can do so if they want to. We're a free people, free to do whatever we want," our guide stated resolutely as we were being driven down the serpentine road away from the church.

"C'mon, people aren't really free to believe whatever they want. In this entire country of over twenty-two million people, how is it that there are only two hundred Christians, and they all happen to attend that one church?" I asked skeptically.

"We live very comfortably under the leadership of our Great Leader, so there's no need for churches. If there aren't any church goers, why should we waste our time constructing such buildings? We can't force people to attend something that they don't want to participate in." He paused for a moment to light a cigarette.

"During the Korean War, the Americans bombed Pyong Yang. The entire city was destroyed. Pyong Yang's population at the time was four hundred thousand. The Americans dropped a thousand pounds of bombs per person, two hundred thousand tons in all. Their bombs destroyed all of our church buildings. Since they're the ones who presumably first taught other nations about God, who the heck would want to believe in such a God after that?" He took a long drag from his cigarette.

Before the Korean War, over 1,530 churches were in existence in the Northern Peninsula alone—the region today known as North Korea. Not one church was left standing after the war ended. It was not until 1988 that another church was built: the Bongsu Church. Today there are three Christian churches in existence in North Korea; of course, all are located in Pyong Yang: the Bongsu Church, the Chilgol Church, and the Jangchung Church.

Whether we are to believe any of their claims of religious freedoms or whether the churches simply exist as an elaborate prop in a sinister display of show and tell to satiate foreigners' curiosities, one thing is clearly evident: these three churches would not exist in North Korea without the Lord's mighty power at work.

Cherishing Freedom

Dr. Chang and I spent five nights and six days in North Korea. During that time we frequently, heatedly debated with some of the North Korean officials assigned to accompany us. This was due mostly to their unrelenting attempts to indoctrinate us with lengthy monologues about Juche and our stubborn opposition to these.

"We've lived in the U.S. for over thirty years. We value individual lives and personal freedom. How is it that you expect us to change our beliefs and simply accept your explanations of Juche as being unequivocally true?" I said defiantly.

"We don't know. We're only doing our job. Sit down and listen!"

The day of our departure, those same officials who had so intensely argued against us, came to Pyong Yang Airport to see us off. "Stay healthy, and please come again," said one of the government guides as his eyes welled with tears.

We said our goodbyes and hugged one another. These men appeared to be so naïve, not unlike children living in a secluded and remote country, alienated far from reality. My heart went out to them.

We returned to Beijing, China. "Ah! We've made it! We've come back to the free world alive. Thank you, Lord!" I had never quite cherished the feeling of freedom as much as I did that day. My spirit had felt heavy and oppressed in North Korea. In China—another spiritually oppressive country—I felt free, light, relieved, and exhausted. Upon returning to our hotel room, Dr. Chang and I immediately fell asleep. We were both unconscious before our heads hit the pillows.

It was not until the next morning that I made a call home. My anxious wife answered the phone. "Where are you? Is it okay for you to call?"

"Yes, I'm fine. I'm in Beijing."

"Are you saying that you still haven't left for North Korea?"

"No. We returned from North Korea yesterday."

There was brief silence. I suddenly remembered that I had promised to call the *second* I returned from North Korea, but had forgotten to do so. "I'm sorry. When we got back, we were so exhausted that we practically collapsed into bed."

She sighed in relief. "Well, when I didn't hear from you on the day you were *supposed* to call, I began thinking that maybe you had been detained. I asked many people to pray for you and Dr. Chang."

Ah, thanks to all those prayers, Dr. Chang and I not only returned safely, we slept soundly.

Wooing the Most Unlovable Woman

April 1989. I began thinking of ways to collaborate with other doctors to effectively pursue North Korean medical missions. With forty-seven Korean-American Christian doctors in Detroit—many of whom had participated in the world mission prayer meetings with me and my wife—I founded the Christian Association for Medical Missions (CAMM). Fervently, we worked to enlist more and more members, and participation in our mission gradually increased to well over a hundred physicians. Doctors joined from many major cities across the fruited plains: Chicago, Boston, New York, Atlanta, Buffalo, and Los Angeles.

Here in the U.S., increasing polarity regarding the issue of providing aid to North Korea had intensified and we found ourselves working against a rising tide of public opinion. Skeptics warned that we would be used, manipulated, and owned by the North Korean government. Others commented that it was too risky an endeavor to work inside a country such as North Korea.

Undeterred, I brainstormed items that the North Korean government *could not* manipulate into weapons of war. Our goal was to impact the masses through medicine. Therefore, CAMM's first official project became the sending of updated medical journals and texts to North Korean medical personnel. We collected medical publications: books, papers, research studies, magazines—the best available, anything and everything we could get our hands on. We eventually amassed over two thousand medical books and five thousand professional journals. The unanimous decision was made to stamp our organization name, "Christian Association for Medical Missions," on the inside of each of the collected books and magazines, with the hope that the words *Christian* and *Mission* would evoke a curiosity and lead to the opening of hearts in those who read them.

We determined that it would be necessary to stamp more than one page. If only the cover pages were stamped, the North Korean authorities could easily locate and tear out those offending pages before distributing the books. Therefore, in addition to the cover pages, we also stamped random pages throughout each of the publications. For two weeks we rotated, several of us gathering together each evening at one of our homes, after a full, exhausting day at work, to methodically stamp each book. We prayed and sang praises as we worked: "Dear Lord, please allow anyone who sees these stamped words to meet you as their Lord and Savior."

We jumped through numerous hurdles to send a forty-foot shipping container full of these books to North Korea. The U.S. State Department, the South Korean CIA, and the North Korean government each led us through lengthy and cumbersome approval processes. Generous expenditures of energy, effort, and patience were necessary in persuading all three agencies of our true and sincere motives to aid the North Korean people. Eventually, approvals came through from each, and with prayerful hearts and soaring spirits, we sent the books.

A few months later, I received a phone call. "DIDN'T WE TELL YOU NOT TO USE SUCH WORDS AS *CHRISTIAN* OR *MISSION*? HOW COULD YOU STAMP EVERY BOOK? ARE YOU CHRISTIAN SPIES? DO YOU WANT TO SEE ME DEAD? WE TOSSED AWAY ALL THE BOOKS YOU SENT INTO THE OCEAN!" screamed a North Korean official.

His words struck me like a swift kick to the gut. How could they do that to all those books we had so laboriously collected? I could already see the fallen faces of our disappointed organization members. Not even cognizant of doing so, I protested angrily to the Lord, "Father, how could this have happened? *You* were the one who led us there. *You* were the one who instructed us to help those people. So, how could this have happened? "

Seething in self pity, it slowly dawned on me that we had worked with a fatal blind spot in our understanding and expectations. Fully aware of the North Korean government's prohibitive stance on religion, their response should have been easily expected. If we were ever going to reach these people, we would need to place ourselves in their position and anticipate their responses more wisely.

God was unveiling the steps to an intricate tango, to woo and win over the heart of the most hardened woman. North Korea was surely the most reclusive, the most difficult of nations to win over for the Lord. But, that was exactly what He wanted us to do.

Medical books/ journals to send to North Korea

Our Wish Is Unification

Spring 1989. Eight members from CAMM, accompanied me into North Korea for the second time to conduct negotiations with the North Korean government regarding the possibility of building a hospital in Pyong Yang. Our flight itinerary was such that it had us stopping in Tokyo first, then Beijing, and from there to North Korea.

I disliked being in Beijing. The proud, ubiquitous displays of the red Chinese flag, coupled with a heavy military presence in the city, were forceful, double-faceted reminders of communism. I found it all very oppressive and intimidating.

During our brief layover in Beijing, we decided to search for a Korean restaurant. We found two: one was the Pyong Yang Cold Noodle, a Korean restaurant owned and run by the North Korean government; the other was a Korean restaurant owned by a third-generation Korean-Chinese family.

We chose to visit the Korean-Chinese restaurant. Much to our surprise and delight, the restaurant had a blue tile Korean roof (an ancient architectural style dating back thousands of years). Nostalgic joy filled us when we saw this traditional Korean structure in the middle of Beijing.

A young Korean-Chinese waitress welcomed us warmly as we entered the restaurant. She spoke fluent Korean and even wore a brightly colored traditional Korean garment (*hanbok*). Immediately, we felt at home, elated to be in an atmosphere of familiar food and language while in a foreign land. The restaurant was packed with a dinner crowd, and there was a roaring buzz of nonstop banter. We ordered our favorite Korean soups and specialty dishes and hummed praises as we waited. Fifteen minutes flew by and our food arrived. Relishing our delicious meals, our stresses ebbed away as we relaxed and eased ourselves into a contented comfort.

"Hey, bring us some more side dishes here!" a loud voice hollered abruptly.

We looked in the direction of the loud voice and noticed a table of five North Korean men eating dinner. They were each wearing the identifying Kim Il Sung badges on the left lapels of their jackets. We had not noticed them before.

We froze in silence. The light and joyful ambience we had basked in seconds before vanished instantly. Fear gripped our hearts. At the time, strange news reports had surfaced about mysterious disappearances of ordinary people around the world. According to some agencies, the North Korean government was suspected of carrying out these kidnappings. We rushed to finish what remained of our meal, prodding one another to hurry so that we could leave before any trouble occurred. We no longer wanted to be there or draw unnecessary attention to ourselves.

As we rose from our seats, however, one of my colleagues quite suddenly stopped and without warning began to sing a popular unification song in a loud and booming voice. "Our wish is unification, even in our dreams, our wish is unification, oh come unification . . ."

We looked at him as if he had *literally* lost his mind. Undeterred, he continued to boldly sing. And strangely, as he pressed on with his lunatic acappella, the instinct to flee, which had overwhelmed us seconds ago, dissipated and a desire to join this crazy colleague kicked in. As if on cue, flinging our previous fears to the wind, the rest of us at the table joined in, and together we sang the unification song in loud, boisterous voices.

The five North Korean men who had instilled such terror in us moments before, slowly rose from their table and sauntered over to join us. There in the middle of the restaurant with fellow diners open mouthed and gawking, as if to question our collective sanity, we sang and held each other in embraces as if we were long lost friends—North Koreans and South Koreans together, singing the unification song with all our might. Emotions overtook us and some of my team members began to weep.

"Yes, we must unify the country. We're one nation. Let's be united!" one of the men exclaimed. We sang the song over and over. "Let's meet again after unification!"

We departed the restaurant, emboldened with an avowed commitment for reunification of the two Koreas. Despite the separated histories, differing government structures, and opposing ideologies, South Korea and North Korea were one nation, one people. We must unify!

A few days later we arrived in Pyong Yang, only to encounter a stark dose of reality. The volatile challenge of synchronizing the theory of reunification into actual practice would entail overcoming sixty years worth of deep-rooted oppression and wide, gaping chasms of repressive intimidation.

During our stay, our team was granted permission to interact with some of the North Korean university students. "Why do you think South Korea and North Korea need to be reunified?" I asked of them.

"If you go to South Korea, the rich die of gluttony, the police beat students to death, and American men rape the women. Shouldn't we unify the country to save South Korea?" answered a young man. "Unification will bring prosperity to our nation. Until then, we must tighten our belts and endure every suffering!"

He spoke with complete conviction that his statements were incontrovertible truths. These students had been thoroughly brainwashed into an assimilating mentality to accept such nonsense, as facts. They were willing to sacrifice their lives and freedoms for the sake of "destroying the enemies of North Korea, completing the revolution, and seeing the day of unification when they would be able to enjoy beef soup with rice, plentifully."

The government's main objective was to accelerate its dominance and political power, at all costs. We had a long haul ahead of us. The power of the gospel would be the only answer to breaking through such crushing chains of isolationism and bringing about a healing reunification.

Our team had not come empty handed. We had brought donations of abundant quantities of medicine and medical supplies for the hospitals. The North Korean officials expressed great appreciation.

"Although you stamped all those medical books with Christian words, we remain very thankful to you for keeping your promise to send them. We're also grateful for your efforts to mobilize help and support on our behalf."

We were invited to a dinner at the People's Grand Study Hall in the Grand Central Library, a banquet hall which accommodates up to three thousand students. After dinner, we embarked on a casual tour of the facility and were stunned to discover that all the medical books we had so laboriously sent had not been thrown into the ocean, after all, as the incensed official had claimed, but were actually prominently displayed on shelves in a designated room for "The Most Valuable Books." I perused several of the books and saw that our organization name remained stamped on virtually every page: "Christian Association for Medical Missions."

Yes! Hallelujah! The Lord surely works out all things for the good of those who love Him. Despite the angry officials, the Lord had arranged for the books to be available to North Korean medical staff to read and perhaps become curious, to seek and one day believe.

That evening, I knelt down before the Lord, humbled and in awe of His display of power and amazing grace.

Bongsu Church

During this second trip I visited the Bongsu Church again with my team. Since my last visit, the church had undergone many changes. Plush red carpet had been laid over what was once a bare concrete floor. There was a small choir and an elderly woman accompanist sitting by an old upright piano.

I was asked to introduce my team and share a few words of greetings with the congregation. Excitement and joy stirred within me as I walked up to the pulpit. Here I was in North Korea, sharing the words of our Lord Jesus Christ with people the rest of the world regarded as enemies.

"I'm so delighted to be with you. Despite the fact that we're one people, we're only now meeting after wasting fifty years of needlessly hating each other. We're a medical mission team from America. We've come here to help you and share the Lord's message of love and healing with you. We're all His children. I pray that God's kingdom prevails here on the Korean peninsula. God bless you," I said enthusiastically.

The audience responded with resounding amens and a round of applause. The rest of my team members quickly filed out of the front pews and joined me on stage to sing a hymn we had specially prepared for the congregants. Thoroughly gripped by the momentousness of the unique experience, tears rolled down our faces as we sang.

And, there was no escaping the overwhelming irony that we were praying and singing praises to the Lord, in a land where He supposedly does not exist.

Please Fill the Inside of This Hospital

March 1991. At the North Korean government's behest, Dr. Myung Kyu Yoon—an anesthesiologist and one of my closest friends from medical school—and I made an impromptu trip into Pyong Yang. We were taken straight to a construction site on Kwangbok

Street, in the heart of the capital city. Construction had been halted, and only a skeleton of a building stood in the drizzly rain.

One of the officials pointed to it. "This is supposed to be a five-hundred bed facility. Please fill the inside of this hospital," he said.

Our organization had wanted to build a medical facility in North Korea. We anticipated initially, starting small, perhaps building a clinic. We had never envisioned commencing with a large hospital like this. Dr. Yoon and I stood silently at the edge of the site, as the light rain fell more steadily. The sheer size of the building alone made me feel already overburdened. We were both too well acquainted with the enormity of the task involved in running a hospital this size. How much money would be needed just to complete the construction, alone? This is way beyond our capacity as a small group of doctors. Our answer should be no.

"Father, all I had wished for on my last visit was to build a small clinic for these people. Now what should I do?" I whispered to the Lord. The government officials stood nearby, waiting for our reply.

"It's beyond our capacity" was at the tip of my tongue when the Lord said to me, "If Jehovah pleases . . ."

Suddenly, I realized the burden of accomplishing this task was not on *me* or *us*, but rather on *Him*. It was His project and He would see it through. Amazingly, the Lord prompted the very same thoughts in Dr. Yoon.

Together we gave our answer to the North Korean officials. "Yes, we'll take over this hospital. We'll do our best. It'll have to be accomplished in stages, step by step, depending on how well our fundraising efforts go."

Despite my misgivings, God was keeping me and leading me to accomplish His work.

His will. His way.

4

The Sunshine Policy

Once the commitment to build a full scale hospital in North Korea had been made, CAMM flew into action. Three organization members and I each contributed $10,000 as seed money to jump-start the project we called the "Sharing Love through Medicine" campaign. My weekends were spent visiting different churches around the country in an effort to build partnerships and encourage support for our North Korean hospital. I shared all that I had seen: the suffering, the starving, the vacant hospitals.

"The North Korean people are dying with absolutely no knowledge of who our Lord Jesus Christ is. If we don't help, who will? We're building a charity hospital in North Korea. I urge you to join us in this life-saving endeavor."

Many people lent their support to our mission after hearing me speak. Others, however, questioned my motives. "Are you a Red Communist?" or "What order have you received from North Korea this time?"

It was in part, a reflection of the time and the legacies of the Cold War. Even those individuals supportive of the idea of building a hospital in North Korea expressed concerns: "What if the North Korean government expels you once the hospital becomes operational?" "Wouldn't you just be used and thrown away by them, no matter how hard you work?" "Aren't you being naively manipulated by North Korea, whose scheme is to use you by making you pro-North Korea?"

These possible scenarios concerned me, as well. I appealed to the Lord for enlightenment on the matter. And I was reminded of a story:

> One winter day an elderly man walked on a country road wearing a heavy coat. The sun and the wind watched him. The wind challenged the sun to a contest.
>
> "Let's make a bet."
>
> "On what?"
>
> "Let's see who can get the old man to take off his coat faster."
>
> The sun agreed. "OK. Let's do it."
>
> "I'll go first, you just watch," the wind said confidently, as he blew a mighty gust at the elderly man, trying to whip the coat off of him. However, the old man only wrapped the coat more tightly around himself. The wind tried again and again, but, regardless of how hard he blew, the man tightened the coat more closely. The wind became exhausted and gave up.
>
> It was now the sun's turn. It shined its warmth on him. The elderly man began to sweat and removed his coat. As the sun continued radiating its warmth, the man even took off his shirt. The gentle sun showed its great effect through warmth instead of force.

This is one of Aesop's fables, and the familiar story clicked with me. Yes, the daunting risk of being expelled from North Korea after building and equipping the hospital was all too real. Regardless, the Lord's instruction for us, as Christians, was that we were *not* to repay evil with evil, but rather, with good. If our desire to reach out to those in need was to become paralyzed by fears of being repaid with evil, the evil would have triumphed. The Lord had placed this crucial task before us and it was now our responsibility to faithfully persevere in seeing it through to fruition, irrespective of the outcome.

Were we to be ousted from the country, we would leave behind our own poignant legacy: "Some Christians lovingly and freely gave of themselves to help us without asking for anything in return. When they were expelled from the country, they retreated quietly."

Exemplifying Christ.

In one sense, expulsion would appear as a nefarious defeat. But, if a legacy of our love and kindness was passed on from person to person, the name of our Lord Jesus Christ would ultimately be glorified. Exemplifying Christ's quiet humility, tender loving care, consummate grace, and faithfulness to the end would be the surest way of reaching the suffering masses in North Korea.

Many supported the sunshine approach and helped to facilitate the campaign. This happened in the early 1990s. It turned out to be a forerunner of the North Korean Sunshine Policy adopted by the South Korean government in the late 1990s.

Pouring Water into a Bottomless Vase

My weekends became booked months in advance as more churches across the country invited me to speak to their congregations. With these invitations increasing exponentially, the endeavor to accommodate them all became very costly, as I traveled at my own expense.

Many enthusiastic supporters had joined our fundraising endeavors, and we experienced a steady rise in contributions. However, it was never enough, and we were constantly short of funds. Meanwhile, expenses for our North Korean hospital continued to mount: equipment, supplies, medicine, thousands of items necessary to make a huge hospital operational.

It seemed as if we were pouring water into a bottomless vase.

I became thoroughly exhausted by the nonstop fundraising efforts. One day, out of the blue, I asked my wife, "How about if we sell the building we have in front of my office?"

At first, she looked skeptical. Ah, I understand your reaction, I thought. Our children were still young, and the building was supposed to be part of our retirement plan.

Apparently, I had misunderstood.

"I'm amazed by the Lord's grace. It seems like it was only yesterday that you worked like a maniac to buy that building. But now, you want to give it all away for the Lord. I'm thrilled that you value Jesus and His work so much."

My mouth actually dropped open.

I should not have been too surprised by her response. Since the day we were married, she had never missed her early morning prayers. Not once. Her faith and support lavished me with the assurance to confidently carry on.

We sold the building and added this money to the hospital fund. Even so, we were still deficient. To alleviate these financial difficulties, I wrote personal letters to Korean-American pastors and other Christian leaders throughout the country, asking for their support. I wrote thousands of these letters by hand, and my fingers began to ache from overuse and arthritis.

Many family members of those in our organization became actively involved in the fundraising process. Someone suggested holding a fundraising golf tournament and the idea was unanimously accepted. We sent hand-made invitations to members of the local community, and one hundred twenty people in all participated. It was the first fundraising event staged by our mission.

Doctors Were Meant to Do Missionary Work

South Korea, 1991. "Pastor, do you remember me? My name is Elder Sai Rok Park, and I met you in Detroit many years ago," I said, as I approached a short, trim man with reading glasses perched on his nose.

"Ah, of course, I remember. How could I ever forget the gorgeous house by the lake on the golf course?"

Pastor Kyung Jik Hahn of the Young Rak Church in South Korea—that was how he remembered me. He was one of the many pastors I had met years ago when my wife had invited him to our home for dinner during his visit to Detroit. He held my hands and smiled warmly as I briefly shared my mission endeavors and the progressive manner in which the Lord had been moving in my life. "It must be very difficult to take on all these mission responsibilities with all that you have to do," he stated afterward. "However, I believe doctors, more than anyone, were meant to do missionary work."

The next day, Pastor Hahn invited me to accompany him to a pastors' conference held at the headquarters of a large South Korean nonprofit organization devoted to sending food staples—such as rice and flour—to North Korea. The organization had mobilized hundreds of pastors from across the entire country.

I shared my testimony for the first time in South Korea at this conference, and, after hearing me speak, many of the pastors in attendance extended invitations for me to speak at their respective churches. As I began expanding my travels to churches throughout South Korea, I gained numerous supporters along the way. Ironically, many of the pastors I had begrudgingly met many years ago in Detroit when my wife had invited them to our home against my stern wishes eventually became some of my greatest mission collaborators and colleagues.

The Prayer Mountain

October 1991. I was invited to be the keynote speaker at the World Christian Medical Mission Conference held in South Korea. I arrived in Seoul via North Korea as I had wanted to first check on the progress of the hospital construction that had commenced in March. It was my fourth trip into North Korea. People began warning me of the South Korean CIA's probing investigations into my activities in North Korea. But, I did not concern myself with that so much.

My flight into Seoul had been greatly delayed, and by the time I arrived at Kimpo Airport, the conference at the Choong Hyun Church had already begun. I arrived two hours late and eased into the sanctuary as inconspicuously as I could manage. Suddenly, the entire audience bolted up out of their seats and erupted into an enthusiastic applause, shouting, "Hallelujah! Elder Park has made it!"

"We've been praying for you since the start of the conference because we thought that you had been detained by the North Korean authorities." I was moved beyond words. These people had been praying for me and my safety the entire time they had waited!

It was almost 11:00 p.m. A friend and I headed for the Samgak Mountains for overnight prayers. I was scheduled to give my keynote speech the next day and felt the need to prepare myself in prayer before the Lord. We moved carefully up the rugged mountain trail, passing two middle-aged women also making their way up the rocky path. I figured that there must have been something extremely pressing to pray about for these women to be climbing the rough terrain at that late hour. My curiosity got the best of me. "Good evening," I finally said.

"Good evening."

"Where're you headed?"

"Oh, we're going to the overnight prayer."

"What brings you to the overnight prayer mountain?"

"More than anything else, we're praying for reunification of the two Koreas."

I was floored. I had assumed that they were there to pray about their family lives, husbands, or children. I was even more astonished when we arrived at the hilltop. Dozens of people were fervently praying, kneeling, standing, weeping, in between boulders, behind rocks, trees, all over the hillside and ravine. People were crying out to the Lord, asking *specifically* for Korean reunification. The entire area reverberated with sonorous prayers pleading for reunification.

Look at all these people praying for the nation! This is why South Korea is so blessed, I thought. If we keep praying like this, the two Koreas will reunite for sure. Bless all these people praying through the night. I'm so ashamed. I seldom pray for reunification. Not like these people. Yet, wherever I go, people call me a man of faith, a pioneering missionary for North Korea. I'm so ashamed.

Surrounded by the palpable, electrifying synergy of prayers, I pleaded and cried out to the Lord. "Dear Father, you have brought me along up to this point. Show me how to keep going. Help me to rise on my feet even though I'm weak and unworthy! May your will be my will. May your words be my words."

I prayed through the night and in the morning descended the mountain as the sun's pinkish hues began peeking through the trees. I felt warm inside, blessed with His grace.

At 10:00 a.m. I gave my keynote speech. It was hardly an easy endeavor to raise funds in South Korea for a North Korean hospital. Grim memories of the Korean War remained bitterly raw in the minds of many South Koreans. Many church leaders had come from the northern provinces, barely escaping with their lives from the North's communist persecution. The raging prevalence of anti-communist sentiment in South Korea at that time equated the term *North Korea* with subversion and espionage. Under the circumstances, it was difficult to preach "love your enemies." Yet, I believed that it was right and good for us to bless our suffering brothers and sisters with selfless deeds of love and kindness.

> **"Be not overcome by evil, but overcome evil with good"**
> **(Romans 12:21).**

Responses to my testimony were enthusiastic, and many people agreed to help our mission. In particular, many pastors promised to partner with us.

"Dr. Park!" someone called me from behind. These were new faces. "We'd like to talk to you. We're from the South Korean CIA. We came to monitor you and, if necessary, stop you from speaking at this meeting, but we were deeply impressed and moved by your testimony."

Ah! The Lord has heard my prayers! He is pleased with this work!

From then on, I became more confident. I crossed the Pacific with more frequency, sharing my testimony as more churches became active partners in the building of our North Korean hospital.

God Uses Even Cowards

February 1992. My testimonies began drawing more attention and curiosity to our mission work as I spoke at more churches on both sides of the Pacific. In particular, the North Korean government began keeping surveillance on not only our organization's activities, but also on me.

My dealings with the South Korean media added new complications to the mix. Whether hearing my testimonies in a church or conducting a scheduled interview, whether written or spoken, reporters tended to take great liberties in exaggerating my words, twisting my descriptions, writing half-truths and outright lies. I refused to cater to anyone or speak anything other than the truth. I stayed true to myself and spoke honestly of North Korea and what I observed. Given my upbringing, I was clearly opposed to communism. I always stressed that I, like the rest of the world, had limited access to the country and that my understanding was based solely on my personal experiences and judgments.

My CAMM colleagues and I were scheduled to go back into North Korea to check on the progress of the hospital. I spent the week prior to that trip in South Korea, meeting with a number of pastors from large churches and granting interviews with several South Korean newspapers. The interviews were conducted on the condition that articles could not appear in print until my team and I had returned from North Korea. The night before our departure, I spoke at the South Korean Seoul Church evening service.

We deplaned and entered Pyong Yang Airport. We expected to be greeted by the familiar faces of our government guides warmly welcoming us back. However, that morning, in stark contrast to our previous visits, we received only the cold, stony stares of the North Korean officials. One of them proceeded to step forward and shove a South Korean newspaper in my face. There was a large picture of me on the front page. It appeared that some of the reporters had broken their promise.

I swallowed slowly and attempted to explain. "I did a few interviews in Seoul, but I have absolutely no control over what those reporters write in their papers. Half the time they don't write with accuracy anyway."

"We know that you talked crap at the South Seoul Church last night—how awful the hospitals are in Pyong Yang, how withered the people look, and how starving women are forced to grind cement for roads in the cold. How dare you say such things!" one of the officials seethed.

How could the North Korean government have known what I had shared in a South Korean church last night? I realized that they must have had one of their agents attend the service.

"Look, I have absolutely no control over what those reporters write," I repeated. The official's anger, however, raged unabated, and it was then that I knew that we were in a very dicey position.

That night I was unable to sleep. My imagination ran wild as chills raced up and down my spine at the slightest noise outside my hotel room. I did my best to appear unfazed and maintain an appearance of a strong, calm, composed leader, lest my mission colleagues become nervous. I tried to remain decisive in my dealings with the North Korean officials and made demands of them with an air of confidence that surprised even me. Certainly, I did my best to sound much braver than I felt.

"We brought flour, noodles, and medicine. We want to go and help the flood victims. Please take us there now!" "How long do we have to wait here for approval? We have no time to waste!" "We have to do this now! We're leaving in two days!" With an authoritative tone of voice, I made my requests. Some of my mission colleagues became concerned and asked, "Are you sure you want to be talking to them in that manner?"

Our stay in North Korea was brief and our schedule tight, but it took an excruciatingly long while for us to obtain permission to go anywhere or do anything. Our government guides always had to first procure directives and consent from higher level officials. Four days began to feel like forty.

The day of our departure a dark foreboding sense of danger plagued me, and uneasiness settled heavily into my spirit. Waves of terror swept over me at the mere sight of North Korean soldiers roaming the airport. I was sure that at any moment, someone was going to grab me by the arm and say, "You are not permitted to board this plane. Come with us." Waiting in the plane for clearance to take off was desperately agonizing. Minutes stretched slowly into a macabre stillness. Hurry up and take off! I just knew that someone was coming to force me off the airplane.

Only when the plane finally took off did I feel a crushing weight suddenly lift, and I was able to breathe freely again. The fear had been palpable, as my colleagues too had felt equally nervous.

It was some time later that I learned that the North Korean authorities had actually wanted to detain me, but decided against doing so to avoid provoking further negative public opinion in the U.S.

against North Korea. Additionally, they did not want to jeopardize the completion of the hospital construction in any way.

I was quickly learning that North Korean missions was not for the fainthearted, and I, actually, was born a coward. Growing up, in fact, I would often hear my mother say, "He's a coward. It would have been better for him if he'd been born a girl." Frankly, it was difficult for me to appear as a bold leader and keep my co-workers from losing heart, especially in times of crises.

However, as my walk with the Lord continues to deepen, so does my ability to draw my confidence, security, and strength from Him. I know that Jesus walks with me, and my assurance in His words keeps me strong.

"I am the resurrection and the life. He who believes in me shall live again, even though he dies; and whoever lives and believes in me will never die." (John 11:25-26)

I am often told, "Dr. Park, you have a lot of guts," referring to my seemingly brazen dealings with the North Korean government and frequent trips into the isolated country. My reply is always, "No, actually, I don't have a lot of guts. But my guts seem to have become swollen, thanks to the love of our Lord Jesus Christ."

The Powerful Right Hook of Jesus

It was not easy for me to balance my hospital duties while traveling so often for North Korean missions. Simply put, there was nothing simple about North Korean missions. Getting there was even an arduous task. At that time there were no direct flights from the U.S. to Beijing. To travel from Detroit to Pyong Yang entailed taking flights from Detroit to Tokyo, from Tokyo to Beijing, and from Beijing to Pyong Yang.

Before any of my trips into North Korea, I usually conducted clinics, seeing patients throughout the day before catching my flight for Tokyo in the evening. On one particular trip, I boarded my

Tokyo flight feeling overworked and tired. While waiting in Tokyo for my Beijing flight, I began to feel ill. By the time I boarded the plane, I was running a fever, accompanied by body aches and chills. I sat in my seat, shivering under several layers of blankets, grumbling complaints under my breath. I was miserable and sick and found it wonderfully convenient to place the blame for all my troubles on my wife's shoulders. So many beautiful young ladies were after me when I worked at the hospitals in Korea, but I had to end up marrying a prayer fanatic! Had I not met my wife, my life would have been so nice and comfortable. It's all because of her that I got into this North Korean mission work to begin with and now I'm suffering for it!

God became my next target. "Heavenly Father, how could you allow me to fall ill like this when you know what I'm trying to do and where I'm going. Haven't I done enough for North Korea? Let me stop. I don't feel like continuing. I hate going there. It's oppressive. It's stifling. And I'm sick and tired of everything!"

I was drowning in my own gloomy pool of disappointment and self-pity when a humble-looking young Caucasian man cautiously approached me. "Would you happen to know what this book is?" he asked as he showed me a pocket-sized book in his hand.

I was not in the mood for conversation with him or anyone else. "I'm not feeling well and I don't feel like talking right now. Please leave me alone!" I said dismissively.

He flushed and looked highly embarrassed. He quietly returned to his seat. A few minutes later, I heard him say, "Amen, Hallelujah!"

It woke up my spirit. I sat up, leaned over, and asked him, "Uh, excuse me, what book is it that you were trying to show me?"

"It's the Bible. You looked like you were in pain and I thought that you might want some encouragement. I just finished praying for you. Have you ever thought about attending church?"

I was stunned by his words and at a loss as to what to say next. Businessmen frequently traveled to China from the U.S., and I had just assumed that he was also one. I thought the book that he had been holding was an English-Chinese dictionary.

"I'm . . . I'm a Christian, too," I stammered foolishly. "I'm . . . uh . . . actually on a mission trip to North Korea, although I'm not feeling well. My Bible is in my bag, unfortunately." I felt greatly ashamed of myself as I spoke.

Though I was traveling on a mission trip, I had tucked my Bible inside my carryon bag and stowed it away in one of the overhead bins. I immediately got up out of my seat and retrieved my Bible. Boy, my true colors were being revealed on this trip! People often addressed me as a dear doctor, professor, missionary, or pastor, but in the face of a small difficulty, I didn't look to the Bible or to the Lord for comfort. Instead, I shifted the blame onto my poor, innocent wife.

The young man and I began sharing our individual journeys of faith with each other. He then read me some of his favorite Bible verses:

> *Through faith we are shielded by God's power until the coming of the salvation that is ready to be revealed in the last time. In this you greatly rejoice, though now for a little while you may have had to suffer grief in all kinds of trials. These have come so that your faith—of greater worth than gold, which perishes even though refined by fire—may be proved genuine and may result in praise, glory and honor when Jesus Christ is revealed.*
> *(1 Peter 1:5–7)*

I had studied theology for many years and had even taught a class in mission studies at a theological seminary. Yet, I had never recognized the true splendor of the book of 1 Peter. My mind became electrified and I felt energized as the Lord's encouraging words of comfort flowed over me like a serene river of tranquility and rest.

Sensing the Holy Spirit's presence around us, deep regret and repentance for my selfishness sprang up within me. I also read a passage of Scripture for the young man. He and I then prayed for each other.

The landing announcement came, and I was surprised at how quickly four hours and thirty minutes had zipped by. My body felt refreshed and my spirit renewed. The Holy Spirit had replaced my pain with peace and had bathed away my sour attitude.

The doors opened and people bustled to get off the plane. The young man walked rapidly ahead. Wishing to keep in touch, I called out to him, "Hello! Hello!"

He turned around.

"Please give me your name and phone number. I'd like to keep in touch with you."

He replied gently, "You don't have to remember my name, and I don't have to remember yours. Those are things of this world, things that will perish. Just remember the verse I taught you. I'll remember the verse you taught me, and someday, we'll meet each other in heaven. We'll remember each other through the verses we shared today."

I was in awe. I felt as if I had been hit with a big blow. It was the most powerful right hook to land on me in all my fifty years of life. I literally staggered and struggled to regain my balance. I tried to catch him, but he disappeared through the bustling crowds of people.

Then I realized that it was Jesus who had come to reassure me. Jesus is always with us, comforting us through our troubled times, instilling hope when we lose it, and gently lifting us back to our feet when we fall. I had been complaining about the difficulties I was facing, and Jesus gave me the assuaging words of the Holy Spirit through a humble young man. Although I was slow to realize it, the Lord did not want me to focus on this particular man or the world.

He wanted me to focus on Him.

The Stormy Sea of Frustration

With funds raised through the "Sharing Love through Medicine" campaign, the construction of the North Korean hospital had been completed, and we began slowly filling the hospital with necessary equipment and supplies. The list was endless: five hundred beds, equipment for two obstetrical delivery rooms, three operating rooms, emergency rooms, internal medicine department, pediatrics department, gynecology department, medicines, supplies, equipment. In short, we needed a lot of help.

I began arranging visits to North Korea for as many people as possible in the hopes of stimulating participation for our mission. Usually ten to fifteen people joined our CAMM members for each trip into the isolated country.

However, as is often the case, many people had ulterior motives for wanting to travel into North Korea. Some went in search of long-lost family members separated for nearly fifty years. Some went out of sheer curiosity. And others went for personal ambition, gain, or greed. Consequently, instead of increasing support and active participation for our mission, I was often left to deal with a bizarre myriad of complications unrelated to our mission.

To add to our difficulties, no ship or airliner offered any cargo service to North Korea at the time, and for a while we transported the medical equipment and supplies in person. This often meant that we literally carried them on our shoulders through airports.

Sympathizing with our cause, Northwest Airlines generously transported our cargo without any extra charge. Unbelievably, the North Korean airliners would always charge us fees for carrying on extra cargo. We would protest, "We're bringing the medicine and supplies to help *your* people. We're giving these items to your country free of cost. You shouldn't be charging us. The money we're paying you in cargo fees could be spent on bringing more medical goods to help your people next time."

The response was always the same. "Don't argue with us, and don't ask us any questions. If you bring on any cargo on our planes, you have to pay fees."

Additionally, dealing with the North Korean authorities was increasingly difficult and frustrating beyond comprehension. Though anxious for our assistance, the officials placed severe restrictions on our movements and actions, keeping us tightly constrained within the unyielding parameters of North Korean governmental policies. They kept biting the hand that was attempting to feed them.

If we brought one shipping container of something, they would demand two. If we brought four, they wanted five. When we arrived in North Korea, we often faced haughty, ungrateful, arrogant, and demanding officials:

"What is the monetary value of these items?"

"Why didn't you bring American-made products instead of products made in South Korea?"

"How come you brought used goods instead of brand new products?"

If we even dared to look bewildered, they would taunt us:

"Who told you we needed your help? We don't need your help!"

"When did we ever ask you to give us these goods in the first place?"

"Get out of here! Go back home and leave us alone!"

Sometimes, exasperation filled me to the point of quitting. Many times I felt like screaming, "Dear Lord, why do I have to accept such abuse from people I'm trying to help?" However, quitting was never an option.

Instead, we did our best to reason kindly with the officials: "Please accept these for your people who are in desperate need of them. Let's first save lives." We did our best to appeal to them: "Shouldn't we first and foremost save lives so that there can someday be reunification, a united Korea?"

Lastly, we remained steadfast as we knew that Jesus wept for the poor and suffering North Korean people. Because of His love for them, He had sent us. Because He cared, we had to care and could not quit.

Due to the Lord's embracing love, we squelched our pride, subdued our discouragement, and did our best to embrace the thankless and haughty officials lovingly, as apostles of the Lord. Our enduring strength and tenacity came solely from the Lord, who showed us that we would not drown in our stormy sea of frustration and exasperation, so long as our eyes remained focused on Him.

Yuhoon Hospital

We had wrangled with the North Korean officials over the name of the hospital. Originally, it had been called the Kim Il Sung Revolutionary Fighter Hospital when the construction had first started. After our organization had taken over the construction, we demanded a new name and asked them to choose one among the following: Love Hospital; Peace Hospital; Luke Hospital; Unification Hospital.

The North Korean authorities rejected our choices and suggested that we name it the Third Hospital instead. We agreed. Since the First and Second Hospitals already existed in Pyong Yang, the name seemed neutral. I regarded the hospital as God's own, owned neither by CAMM or the North Korean government. I personally felt happier about the name. Our North Korean hospital was officially called the Pyong Yang Third Hospital. However, North Korean officials also had another name for the hospital: The Yuhoon Hospital. It was so named because of President Kim Il Sung's directive before he passed away: the Yuhoon Directive.

He had left instructions to the North Korean hierarchy "to do their best to cooperate in the completion of the Pyong Yang Third Hospital and appreciate the love for the fatherland displayed by the

Korean American doctors." North Korean officials later explained that new directives issued by President Kim Il Sung must be learned and memorized by every North Korean citizen each week. It was mandatory.

President Kim Il Sung's Yuhoon Directive: "Dr. Sai Rok Park and the Korean-American doctors who love the fatherland have helped to build and open the Pyong Yang Third Hospital. Appreciate the love for the fatherland displayed by these Korean-American doctors."

Not long after this directive was issued, my colleagues and I were granted permission to visit Sariwon—a rural province located two hours outside of Pyong Yang. I had promised a friend from the U.S. that I would help locate his younger sister and brother, who were rumored to be living there. I also had relatives in North Korea on my mother's side—my family used to live in Wonsan—but had not tried to find them. This was not due to a lack of interest; I felt that it was imperative for me to remain focused on the Lord's will while in North Korea. I did not want to dilute my attention and energy in any way for a personal agenda. Nevertheless, I could not look the other way when other Korean-Americans asked me to assist them in the search for their families.

As it turned out, my friend's sister and brother were living in Sariwon and had been easily located. Arrangements were made for us to meet them there. We arrived at the designated village, and I was puzzled to see a shriveled and frail-looking elderly woman waiting for us. Ah, I guess, we're going to be meeting my friend's mother instead of his sister, I thought to myself. One of the government officials brought her over to us. "This is the doctor from America," he announced.

The old woman asked us feebly, "Do you know Dr. Sai Rok Park who has done wonderful work for our fatherland?"

"This is he." The official pointed to me.

The old woman grasped my hands and burst into tears.

I was taken aback by her reaction and then realized that she knew of me, knew of us, through President Kim Il Sung's Yuhoon Directive. It was at that moment that I realized the power behind those presidential directives. Every North Korean citizen had to memorize those directives each week, even this poor, frail-looking woman living in this decrepit village.

"How is my older brother in America?" she asked.

Her question startled us. What did she mean, "My older brother?" The woman looked too elderly and weathered to be my friend's *younger* sister. She looked to be a woman in her eighties, and my friend, her older brother, had just turned fifty.

However, she was indeed his younger sister and I felt deeply saddened. She must have endured a lifetime of extreme hardship and suffering to have aged so rapidly.

She introduced me to an elderly man standing next to her, as her youngest brother. It was apparent that he was afflicted with advanced tuberculosis.

"Dear doctor, since you've done wonderful things for the fatherland, you must have the ears of high government officials. My brother is dying. His illness is so serious that he coughs up blood every night. However, he's required to report to work at a very dusty steel factory. Please help him to get a job at a better place," the old woman pleaded tearfully.

As she wept, one of our government guides assured me that he would do his best to secure the sick man a better position.

I have not been able to confirm whether or not the official kept his word.

If We Do Not Help These People, No One Else Will

The following year, a series of natural disasters, droughts, and ravaging floods plundered through North Korea. These events plunged the country more abysmally into the deadly clutches of its already existing famine. Within a few days, our organization raised $200,000, and with those funds we purchased thousands of intravenous fluid bottles, antibiotics, and three hundred thousand instant noodle packets. With urgency, we flew to Pyong Yang.

"The drought and flood affected only a few areas. Most of the provinces around the country are just fine," a North Korean official stated casually. His fellow countrymen were wrestling with life and death perils and yet, his overstated indifference highlighted a diabolical perversion in North Korean logic in which saving the nation's pride in the face of a tragedy overrode saving the nation's lives.

According to United Nations reports, two million people had already starved to death with an equal number of the population barely surviving. The North Korean officials seemed to be in denial. They also threw unbelievable statements at us: "If only one million soldiers and two million Pyong Yang residents survive, we'll still triumph even if the rest of the country starves to death."

"We don't need your help. Who asked you for it? Why do you keep bothering us?" "If you want to help, just leave the supplies here and go back home. We'll take care of the distribution process ourselves."

With dogged persistence and unrelenting determination bordering on obstinacy, we finally managed to obtain permission to take our medical products and food personally to Munduck, one of the largest rice field communities that had been devastated by the floods. The disaster had turned the entire village into a vast wasteland. We were horrified to see people in the streets, sick and starving. We insisted on treating the villagers with the medicine and supplies we had brought with us, but the government officials would not allow us anywhere near the residents or to have any interaction with them.

"We'll take care of our own. You just leave those things here and go," the officials ordered flatly.

"Why can't we help the patients?" we pleaded. But it was pointless to argue. The officials would not relent.

We left the town in anguished tears, our heavy hearts grieving for the people we had seen mired in wretched misery. I promised myself that I would do everything within my power to help these people, as the North Korean officials did not seem motivated to save their own countrymen. As we were driven back into Pyong Yang, I was once again reminded of the old woman and her ill brother from Sariwon.

We have to help these people, I thought. If we don't save them, no one else will.

On my return to the U.S., I made a brief stop at Seoul to share my testimony at one of South Korea's largest churches. "Let's help the North Korean people. Let's help save them physically and spiritually!" I said to the congregation.

At first the church fired up and enthusiastically committed to getting involved with our mission, but their zeal quickly fizzled. They did not want to involve themselves in someone else's mission work; they ultimately wanted a North Korean project in their own name.

As an organization, we were on our own. There was no one to help us and no one for us to depend on.

Five Hundred Hospital Beds

One of our biggest challenges was logistics—how to transport hospital beds to North Korea. Five hundred of them. Due to shipping complications and costs, we purchased the beds in South Korea rather than the U.S. However, even from South Korea, there was no easy way to economically transport them to Pyong Yang.

Our purchased beds sat piled up at Inchon Harbor. I met with a South Korean government official. "Our organization has purchased five hundred beds for the Pyong Yang Third Hospital. Is there any way to obtain government approval and assistance in transporting them into North Korea? This is, after all, a humanitarian Christian mission to save lives. Can the South Korean government help us?"

"Yes, we'll do our best to help you," the official assured me.

"There's one problem. The beds are so bulky and heavy that to ship them would be an astronomical cost. Would it be possible for us to send them through the DMZ?" I asked. The DMZ (Demilitarized Zone) is the massively fortified border between South Korea and North Korea. It is the most heavily militarized border in the world.

"To do that, you first need to obtain North Korea's acceptance of your proposal," the official stated.

On that note, I rushed to Pyong Yang.

The North Korean officials gave me a similar response. "We'll only go along with this transport method if South Korea agrees to it first. And then, they need to promise to send the beds to us in secret. No one in the public sector can know about it."

I flew back to Seoul.

"First of all, the approval has to come from the North. If they say yes, we'll agree to it, too. Secondly, keeping this hidden from the media in a free country is next to impossible. We can do our best, but certainly can't promise anything," the South Korean official stated dubiously.

I lobbied between the two countries, bouncing back and forth like a ping pong ball, expending much energy and losing valuable time. We continued to search for other alternatives and began holding prayer meetings every morning in front of the five hundred beds piled up at Inchon Harbor.

"Dear Lord, please give us a way to transport these hospital beds to Pyong Yang."

Two weeks of prayer and still no answer. We started getting nervous about the weather, especially rain. We were running out of time.

Finally, we determined that it would be most economical for us to ship the beds to the U.S., from there they would be shipped to the Netherlands, then to Hong Kong, then to Daryon Harbor, and finally to Nampo, North Korea. By the time the beds arrived in

North Korea, they would have traveled a convoluted path across the globe for six months. We saw no other alternative. In the meantime, I returned home due to work obligations.

Not long afterward, I received a mysterious phone call. It was from the captain of a Honduras commercial cargo ship engaged in clandestine shipping business with North Korea. He informed me that a shipment he was supposed to pick up had suddenly been cancelled without prior notice.

"I've heard that you people have been holding prayer meetings at Inchon Harbor, hoping to ship some hospital beds to Pyong Yang. Since we'll be sailing empty to Pyong Yang from Inchon anyway, we'll deliver them for you, free of charge."

I had no idea why his original shipment had been cancelled, but I believed that this was no coincidence.

"Thank you, dear Lord! Everything indeed is in your hands."

With this "parting of the Red Sea" miracle, the beds arrived in Nampo, North Korea, in three days instead of six months. At no cost.

Nothing is impossible for our Almighty God!

Shortly thereafter we received generous donations from other partnering organizations, including $100,000 from World Vision, which expanded our capacity to send medical equipment, goods, and supplies in furnishing the hospital.

The Pyong Yang Third Hospital was a dazzling display of the Lord's limitless ability to make a way, where there was no way.

God Opens the Pyong Yang Third Hospital

November 22, 1995. My colleagues and I spent time in the morning inspecting the Pyong Yang Third Hospital, just before the start of the opening ceremony. We noticed that the beds were missing covers. "Where are the blankets?" I asked the maintenance manager.

"Those worthless things! How could you send us such cheap blankets?" he hissed.

I was quite taken aback. We had sent over five hundred blankets from our supporters in South Korea. "Let me see the blankets," I insisted. "What do they look like? Why are you saying they're worthless?"

"We threw them all away!"

"Bring them out here right now. If you don't bring them out, I'll postpone this opening ceremony," I demanded.

Two thousand people had gathered outside in celebration of the opening of the Pyong Yang Third Hospital. He moved slowly, disappearing down the hallway and reappeared minutes later, clutching one of the blankets.

The blankets were, in fact, of very high quality, thick, beautiful royal blue, silky in texture, with no defects at all. The manager looked highly embarrassed. People were waiting, the ceremony was about to begin.

"Didn't you originally promise to send blankets without the labels 'Made in South Korea'? Three of the blankets still had such labels on them. Don't you know that could cost me my head?"

That was it. They were worried about exposing the fallacies of their notorious propaganda portraying South Korea as a greatly impoverished nation. I left the issue alone and did not press him any further. This incident was just a small illustration of the oppositional challenges of working in North Korea.

Six years after I had first envisioned establishing a hospital in North Korea and four years of painstaking negotiations, fundraising, construction, and equipping, the Pyong Yang Third Hospital was officially opened.

Four of my medical colleagues from the U.S. and Pastor Dong Won Lee from South Korea were among the two thousand attendees. As we proceeded through the tape cutting ceremony, tears of joy flooded my eyes. Afterward nine of us—including three North Korean pastors—conducted a small worship service in front of the hospital entrance. As we began our service, the thousands of people in attendance minutes before, disappeared, almost instantaneously. I felt so saddened to see this, but continued on with our prayer service, nevertheless.

"Dear Lord, this hospital which you built, finally opened its doors today. Through this hospital, may our North Korean brethren come to know your love and be saved. May your Good News and healing spread throughout this land and reconcile South Korea and North Korea to become a united country in your sight."

I requested permission to officially set up a small worship room in the hospital, but the North Korean officials staunchly refused. The hospital management did offer me an honorary chairman's room—they called me the Pyong Yang Third Hospital's Honorary Chairman—for use in any way I wanted. My colleagues and I contemplated making a movable cross for discreet worship services in the room, but ultimately decided against it. Undeterred, we gathered together in the room that day, lifting our prayers and songs of praise to the Lord. My heart was brimming with hope that the expansion of North Korean missions would go blazingly forth throughout the entire country, ignited from this small worship room as a base.

The Pyong Yang Third Hospital

The Lord's Prayer at the Hall of Eternal Life

My colleagues and I were taken to the Hall of Eternal Life at Keumsu Dongsan. This was the final resting place for the late president Kim Il Sung, a place where he had worked when he was alive—similar to the White House for U.S. presidents. It was turned into a mausoleum so that North Korean citizens could come from all over the country to pay their respects to the deceased leader. On the day we visited, there was a long winding line of people waiting to get inside.

We were treated as VIPs and quickly ushered into the mausoleum, bypassing the long waiting line. At the entrance, a gust of compressed air blew forcefully down on our heads. We were told this was to cleanse our hair and clothes of any dust and germs.

Inside the palatial hall, massive statues and sleek marble fixtures stood towering off to the distance, like silent sentries. Toward the center was a large glass case in which lay the late president wearing a dark suit, resting on a traditional Korean pillow. The corpse was tightly guarded by dozens of armed soldiers with sharp bayonets fixed to their rifles.

"Move together and take a bow at the late president's right side, and then move to the left side of his head and do the same. Don't bow by his feet," our government guide instructed us.

My colleagues and I were at a loss. We had just been instructed to make bows to this man, this idol, under supervision of armed guards. The atmosphere was not one that lent itself to any discussion or questioning of the instructions. Ahead of us, tall Eastern Europeans bowed respectfully to the late president, as directed. It quickly became our turn.

"Now let's take our bow." The officials bowed. My colleagues and I remained stiff, none of us bowing. Quietly, I began reciting the Lord's Prayer. "Our Father who art in heaven . . . Our Father . . . Our Father . . ."

Panic began to cloud my brain, and I suddenly could not remember the words to the prayer that I knew by heart, that I knew like the back of my hand and repeated on a daily basis, morning and night. Duress and fear began mounting and my heart began to race.

As the Lord's Prayer faded from my brain, I thought to myself, I might die here.

The officials nudged me, and I moved obediently to the head side of the president's body. If I die here, I thought, how are my innocent wife and children going to live in this world without me? What if I'm labeled a communist and this causes problems later for my children? How shocked my eighty-year-old mother will be when she hears of my sudden death.

I was nudged again to the left side. The soldiers suddenly raised their rifles in unison as they slammed their hands on their guns.

THUMP!

Oh, Lord! I felt as if I were falling off a cliff. My mind went blank with fear. I could not hear or see anything. My colleagues and I continued to stand stiffly when one of the officials tapped me on the shoulder. I was so startled that I almost screamed.

"We're finished now," he uttered in a low voice.

My colleagues and I raced for the doors.

"Dr. Park, Dr. Park!" Someone called me from behind.

I'm dead for sure! I urgently desired to get out of there, now more than ever. One of the officials approached. "We'd like for you to write some commemorating words in the visitor's book on behalf of your group."

Reluctantly, I walked back into the hall and wrote the following words in the guest book: "I wish that South Korea and North Korea would reach a genuine reconciliation in the very near future."

The official hovered over my shoulder as I wrote. "Why do you mention the reconciliation of South Korea and North Korea? I just asked you to write some commemorating words for our Great Leader?" he growled.

"I don't know anything about such things. I'm only a doctor. What would I know about such affairs!" I snapped.

"Nevertheless . . ." He continued to grumble behind my back as I quickly sprinted out to join my colleagues waiting for me outside. They were greatly relieved to see me come out unharmed. They had begun to worry that I was being detained for our group's refusal to bow. Although we had been badly frightened, thanks to the protection of our Lord Jesus, we had gotten through without having to bow.

It was later that I learned that our actions had indeed caused great commotion behind the scenes. An emergency phone call was placed to top North Korean officials. The topic of conversation: what to do about the five people who stood stiffly, refusing to respectfully bow to the late president?

"Who are they?"

"They're Dr. Sai Rok Park and his company."

"Hmm, that's a little complicated . . ." My name had been mentioned in one of the late president's directives, which meant that caution had to be exercised. "They're Christians. Let them pray instead of bowing!"

After that incident, I was able to openly pray in front of the officials without disruption or repercussions. My stubborn faith in the Lord must have been burdensome to those officials assigned to deal with me. They walked a fine line in having to keep a tight reign on our activities without overreaction and having problems inadvertently ricochet their way.

5

Work at the Pyong Yang Third Hospital Idled

The completion of the Pyong Yang Third Hospital did not signify the end of our organization's involvement. The importance of maintaining ongoing support for the hospital in order for it to remain operational spurred us on with our "Sharing Love through Medicine" campaign with renewed vigor and commitment.

In South Korea, a number of people suggested the following idea: Instead of dealing with churches individually, why not unite them under one organization? Continued and uninterrupted aid to North Korea and the Pyong Yang Third Hospital would require tremendous support. Clearly, there was a need for an organization that could mobilize and unite churches for greater efficiency. In response, my colleagues and I established a new organization and tentatively called it the One Nation Unification Preparation Association. We encouraged churches, friends, and individuals to channel their efforts and resources through this association.

The One Nation Unification Preparation Association changed its name to the United Korean Welfare Mission and obtained its legal status as a nonprofit organization from the Foreign Affairs Ministry of South Korea. I became its international president.

Here in the U.S., CAMM continued the "Sharing Love through Medicine" campaign and managed to secure medical donations with a market value of $1,120,000. We immediately sent $500,000 worth of medicines as a first shipment to the Pyong Yang Third Hospital. We followed that with $200,000 worth of emergency medicine and supplies for patients suffering from contagious diseases. In addition, we sent blankets and flour and many other necessities with support and assistance from many American nonprofit organizations.

However, once the Pyong Yang Third Hospital opened, an unexpected obstacle emerged. The North Korean authorities were denying us free access to the hospital we had so laboriously built and equipped. They tightly controlled our comings and goings and imposed severe restrictions on our visits to the hospital. We had agreed to build the facility expressly for the unencumbered ability to treat the patients ourselves, to have free and uninhibited access to them. We had labored tirelessly for this goal, and now we were not able to serve the people we had originally intended to help.

My colleagues and I quarreled heatedly with the North Korean authorities. "You must give us freedom to perform surgeries and save lives at the hospital!"

We implored. We appealed. We pleaded. We begged. All to no avail. The North Korean officials' attitudes remained impervious, indifferent, and unrelenting.

Our only hope was to pray more fervently to the Lord than ever.

I Am an Underground Christian

My colleagues and I were huddled together in prayer in the lobby of the Koryo Hotel before our departure from Pyong Yang. Someone approached me from behind and quickly pulled me aside to a secluded corner. He glanced around nervously, peering left and right to make sure that no one was following, stalking, or lurking in the shadows. He reached into his pants pocket and retrieved a small, faded piece of paper and showed it to me. I read the following message: We know that in all things, God works for the good of those who love him who have been called according to his purpose.

I had heard reports of the existence of underground churches in North Korea, and I realized that this man was an underground Christian.

"I go up to a hill near my home every month to find these kinds of messages under a rock. I write out ten copies and put them back in the same place the following month," he whispered. He did not know who had put the messages there to begin with and who was receiving the ten copies he wrote out.

He had memorized the verse written on the piece of paper, but did not know that it was from the book of Romans 8:28.

I was inspired by this man. The underground Christians in North Korea had perilously maintained their faith despite years of suffocating rule, hunger, illness, and danger. The underground church was alive despite attempts to eradicate such practices and notions. Our role was becoming even clearer to me. We needed to help keep these people alive, feed them, heal them. All this work was about them—the underground survivors—not me or anyone else. We were not the main characters. They were, and everything was happening in accordance to the Lord's master plan.

Perhaps He intended to one day use our brethren in the North as soldiers of the gospel, to testify their faith as future missionaries. And what a powerful testimony they would have! In the meantime, our job was clear: love them and look after them until that time when they would be able to embark on their own apostolic journeys.

And it is not for me or the churches to show these people the Lord's way. They are already living proof of God's grace. Belief despite oppression. Faith despite persecution. The Lord means for us to be faithful in devoting ourselves to all that He has called us to do. As all things are in His control, He will take care of the outcome.

Dear Father, You See Who I Am

With each of my visits, I had never dared to venture into the country alone. I was always careful to travel with a colleague, an eyewitness to our activities, whether it was to deliver products or attend meetings. Any hint of a rumor insinuating that I had praised or supported any particular political regime or engaged in any impropriety would have caused great problems with my supporters in South Korea and the U.S. If a scandal erupted when I was alone in North Korea, I would have trouble proving otherwise.

One time, however, I did make an urgent, impromptu trip into the country by myself. Absolutely none of my colleagues had been available to accompany me on such short notice. I stayed at our usual hotel, the Koryo Hotel, and was assigned to a room on the twenty-ninth floor. For whatever reason—the lack of other foreign guests or a lack of electricity—when I stepped out of the elevator, the entire floor was pitch black.

That night as I lay down to sleep, fear consumed me. I was so frightened that my body trembled. I felt as if I had been locked in a stifling dungeon. Dark, menacing thoughts raced through my mind and I felt an uneasy sense that someone was waiting on the other side of my door, about to break into my room to take my life.

Why did I come here alone? I lamented. I was being driven mad by my own fear, hearing things, seeing things, imagining things.

"Jesus, please help me! Be with me!" I burst out aloud. I was reminded of people I had seen at church being overly expressive during worship, praying out loud, shouting praises at the top of their lungs, gesturing wildly in demonstrative appeal to the Lord. Whenever I had seen such overt behavior, I had always thought that it was excessive, ostentatious. I did not understand why people had to shout and yell.

What a hypocrite I was! There, alone in my hotel room, in isolated North Korea, I felt such overwhelming terror, that I, too, began shouting out my prayers in urgent petition to the Lord—all night. That is how I survived my night of fear!

The next morning, I had breakfast with six high-ranking North Korean officials. Exhausted, I sat quietly at the table. I had not slept at all and felt like a fatigued mess. Before eating, they asked me to speak a few words of greetings.

I rose slowly from my seat. "I'd like to thank you for your warm welcome and for this breakfast." I quickly sat back down.

The officials looked surprised. "Uh, don't you have that greeting that you do with your hands together. Why don't you do that?"

It took me a few seconds to register that they were actually asking me to pray.

I had never been more ashamed of myself than I was at that moment. I called myself a Christian, believer in God Almighty, creator of heaven and earth. Yet I had forgotten to pray before a meal, only to be reminded to do so by unbelieving North Korean officials.

Faced with a wonderful opportunity to show expressions of praise and worship to the Lord, I sat preoccupied with only myself.

I stood up again. "Dear Father, you see who I am. I'm not worthy of your trust. I'm a worthless person before you. Lord, instead of praying for these people last night, I was so afraid. . . . Nonetheless, you've sent me here to share about your love and mercy, and for that I thank you. I pray the Holy Spirit's covering on these people and this land and that you would bring forth your healing. I pray that you would reunite our broken nation. Unite South Korea and North Korea as one, bathed in your love."

To my utter shock and surprise, I heard a few of them say, "Amen"! I had prayed and praised God in front of North Korean officials on many occasions, but never before had anyone responded with an amen.

The Lord was at work here, despite my fear and faithlessness. I realized once again, that North Korean missions was not of my doing; rather it was the mighty hand of Jehovah making the way.

It was later that I learned that some of these North Korean officials had somehow gained access to travel to the U.S. and attended Sunday worship services during their visits. They had come to think that it was proper etiquette to say amen after a sermon or a prayer.

After this incident, I worked and prayed with confidence, wherever I went and whoever I was with. I prayed with people at meals, visitors at hospitals. Alone or with others.

Fearlessly.

The First Foreign Doctors to Treat Patients in North Korea

Two years after the completion of the Pyong Yang Third Hospital, we were still prohibited from interacting with any of the patients. Those two years were fraught with protracted strife and intense acrimony between the respective sides. The North Korean authorities felt overburdened by my presence and unrelenting demands. I felt tremendously frustrated by their volatile behavior and vague, stalling promises. We lobbied back and forth like this, each of us voicing great displeasure, disappointment, and animus with the other.

Miraculously, the North Korean authorities finally assented and granted our medical team an opportunity to see and treat patients at the hospital. Perhaps their acquiescence was a conciliatory gesture on their part.

On September 27, 1997, my surgical team and I performed surgery on a woman to remove a tumor from her ovary at the Pyong Yang Third Hospital. I met with the patient beforehand. She greeted me with a warm, grateful smile, her eyes brimming with tears. Communism, South Korea, North Korea were no longer divisions between us. There was only trust and appreciation and one person's desire to help another. I promised to do my best for her. We held hands together as we prayed, and I thanked the Lord for providing this opportunity to help her and the other patients at the hospital.

We opened up her abdomen to find that the tumor had practically disappeared. However, her appendix was extremely inflamed and we removed it. Although the surgery turned out to be a relatively simple procedure, it was a historic moment. We officially became the first foreign medical team to perform surgery in North Korea since it had become a sovereign nation.

While my surgical team and I performed the operation, other doctors from our mission treated outpatients for minor procedures. We ended our day by personally meeting every patient at the hospital. Many grasped our hands to thank us. Many wept tears of gratitude, and we wept alongside them.

"Thanks to you, we're being treated here."

"Thanks to you, we're saved."

We saw and treated one hundred seventy patients that day at the Pyong Yang Third Hospital. It had taken more than two years of stunted negotiations and bitter strife and wrangling to do so. We now yearned for the ability to hold worship services at the hospital and create a sound base for sharing the gospel throughout all of North Korea.

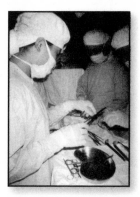

First foreign medical doctors to perform surgery in North Korea

Goodbye, Detroit!

February 1997. I had been praying for a North Korean mission support center in the U.S. My experiences with North Korean medical missions, thus far, had shown me the necessity of having such a center in order to adequately furnish frontline mission fields with medicine and medical supplies more effectively.

While praying for such a center, I received an unexpected suggestion from a pastor. He recommended that we apply to the U.S. government for permission to lease a closed U.S. naval base in Oakland, California, for the purpose of establishing a Christian college and medical welfare center. Four pastors and I gathered together for this task. We submitted a proposal to the federal government, which they accepted.

We were granted permission to lease this land at a cost of $1. I regarded this as God's sure answer to my prayer for a mission support center, and my wife agreed.

We decided to name the Christian school, Pan Pacific University, and as the idea for the school began taking shape, my wife and I made the decision to relocate to Northern California.

Deciding to leave Detroit, which had been our home for over thirty years, was disorienting, to say the least. The Lord was compelling me to make this move, but it was perhaps the most dramatic upheaval of my life. Initially, moving from South Korea to the U.S. had represented an upward mobility, a search for a better life. Leaving Detroit for California represented a rash descent into barrenness; I was relinquishing the privileges and amenities I had enjoyed there and starting over from scratch somewhere else. Also, we would be separated from our children, particularly our youngest son, Andrew, who was still attending school in Detroit.

Two weeks before our departure, we informed the pastor and fellow members of our congregation at the Korean Presbyterian Church of Metro Detroit of our decision. No one could believe it. At the pastor's kind request during a Sunday service, I shared the reason for our departure and expressed deep thanks, appreciation, and love for the members there.

"Well, my friends, I've fought the good fight and kept my faith. It's been seven years since I began leading the early morning Bible studies. I won't be able to continue anymore. As you know, my wife and I are leaving. We want to thank all of you for your love and support. If we've ever disappointed you in any way, please forgive us and cover us with your love and prayers."

Tears flowed.

"We can't imagine our church without Elder and Mrs. Park," people said, embracing us as we left. We had made wonderful friends and strong supporters who had unwaveringly prayed for us since the beginning of our mission.

I also turned in my resignation to Wayne State University Medical School. Learning of my departure, many of my patients broke down into tears. Many of these people had come to trust me not only as their physician but also as their friend. Unsettled as I was to leave them all, I had to be obedient and subject myself to the Lord's grace and guidance. The dean at Wayne State Medical School tried to gently dissuade me. "Even if it is for the sake of Jesus, why would you want to resign from your position? Do you have another job already?" he asked.

"No."

"Then, how are you going to make a living?"

"I don't know."

Concerned, he referred me to the dean at the University of California-Davis Medical School. That was how I eventually acquired my teaching position at UC-Davis Medical School. I was touched by his kind gesture. However, I was not remotely interested in the prospective position; my heart was elsewhere.

"We'll keep your position here open for six months, so come back at any time," he assured me. I knew in my heart that I would not be back, but those words were comforting to hear, nevertheless.

Having resigned from the school, hospital, and church, I finally had the luxury of free time, something of a foreign concept. Up until then, my wife and I had not had time for leisurely travel and I wished to take advantage of the opportunity to cross the U.S. by car. Driving from Detroit to San Francisco seemed exciting and adventurous. I was weary of phone calls, beepers, surgeries, and hospital obligations. I yearned to bask fully in my newly acquired liberty. I longed to visit interesting little towns, eat at quaint, little restaurants, survey mountainous horizons and beautiful scenery along the way without the monotonous weight of stress, pressure and everyday responsibilities. There is an old saying that states, "If a man has vegetables to eat, water to drink, a woman to love, and health to enjoy, there's nothing more to ask for."

I wanted to quiet my hectic life for calm reflection. My soul longed for deep conversation and fellowship with the Lord. While driving day and night under the sun and stars, I wished to hear His voice and know His desires.

My wife was skeptical.

"How can a busy person like you cross the continent by car? Let's just go by plane."

She was being stubborn. She wanted to fly. The trip would be too arduous and tiring, she argued. This time around, however, I would not yield. I was being equally stubborn. There would never be another opportunity to see the beautiful sights around the country.

I managed to persuade her.

Barely.

We shipped most of our belongings through a moving company and loaded up our car in preparation for our week-long, cross-country adventure.

An urgent phone call came through from a church in South Korea requesting my immediate presence to come and lead their revival services. My wife objected strenuously to the idea of me going, but I felt that it was something that I could not refuse. In the end, instead of embarking on the much-anticipated cross-country drive with my wife, I left immediately for South Korea. Our son, Terry, took my place and drove to San Francisco with her, taking the southern route through Texas and New Mexico, enjoying the beautiful sights and picturesque landscapes along the way.

God Who Sends Us Also Keeps Us

I was still in Seoul for the revival services, when my wife found a new place for us in California. With no knowledge of the area, she took out a map and gamely rented the first apartment she saw. When friends at our new church learned of our apartment's location, they frantically advised us to move out of the "dangerous area." We lived there for a year without encountering anything dangerous.

The apartment was a tiny, cramped, basement one-bedroom, with stale air and a lingering smell of mildew. We had no furniture and felt alone and vulnerable in our sparse environment. In moments of weakness, the burden of our seemingly senseless upheaval conjured regretful longing for the comfortable and familiar life we had impulsively abandoned in Detroit.

Additionally, we thought constantly of the children we had left behind. "Should we go back to Detroit?" I asked my wife delicately one evening at dinner as we sat on the bare floor with our rice bowls.

Her face became stern and resolute. "Many missionaries around the world face indescribable hardship. Are we going to complain about this? Shouldn't we be thankful for being sent to this beautiful place?" I was able to find new strength in her words and become refocused.

With ample time on my hands to draw up detailed schedules and plans for the days ahead, I should not have been surprised when nothing went right. First, the deal involving the closed naval base went sour. The U.S. government changed its position and decided against leasing the property to us due to numerous local protestations that arose. The local residents regarded us as foreigners and complained, "Why would you give that beautiful site to foreigners? The citizens here should have it."

Overall, seventeen hearings were held on the matter. It was an ordeal that caused much stress for us all. Passionate appeals were made in attempts to persuade the government officials and the local residents of our project's overall benefit, not only for our mission but also for the entire local community, as well. Ultimately, the government ruled in favor of the local residents, and we were defeated.

It was a stunning blow and I was overwhelmed with ambiguity. I did not know what to do. I had left my entire life in Detroit behind for this project. And now, there was no project. What was I doing here? "Dear Father, I came to California as I believed that this was what you wanted me to do. But now, I don't know what I'm supposed to do. Show me your way. Please guide me."

In the meantime, the sobering reality of everyday responsibilities began to mount. Our large, beautiful home by the lake on the golf course in Michigan, sat on the market with no prospective buyer in sight. Bills began piling up: rent, taxes, water, electricity, mortgage, and I had no income. We eventually sold our home well below the market price. With funds generated from that sale, my wife and I bought ourselves a small home in the Bay Area.

Six months or so had passed when I received a phone call from Wayne State University Medical School. "Your position is still open. But we can't hold it for you any longer. We were hoping that you would return."

Suppressing the instinctive impulse to immediately return to Detroit, I did my best to analyze things objectively. I was unsure of what to do.

We invited our pastor to our home for prayer one evening. "God who sends us also keeps us," he said to me. Those words left a deep impression on me.

After weeks of soul searching, I declined the generous offer from Wayne State Medical School and made the resolute decision to remain in the Bay Area. There is an old Confucius saying that states, "A good horse never eats the grass behind him." I was going to push forward without pausing to look back. My wife seemed very happy with the decision. She had come to enjoy life in the San Francisco Bay Area and believed that the Lord had sent us there for a purpose.

With the passage of time, I began a new position teaching medical students and treating patients at UC-Davis Medical School three days a week. I also headed the gynecology department at the Northern California VA Medical Center. My wife and I were finally starting to carve out a comfortable routine and niche for ourselves.

I am so thankful the Lord saw us through our lonely and stumbled start in California and life in that small one-bedroom apartment in a run-down, gritty neighborhood in a rough part of the city. The Lord's grace and love lifted us through doubtful and befuddling moments.

Thank you, Lord, for carrying us to this day.

6

The Banishment Order

"This order forbids you from entering North Korea. Sai Rok Park is now forbidden to enter North Korea."

The words came at the end of 1997, the second year of the Pyong Yang Third Hospital's opening, when the functioning of the hospital was gradually and finally shifting into full gear.

"What in the world is that supposed to mean?" I asked incredulously.

My alleged crime was "proselytizing Christianity" and "subverting the North Korean policy."

"Am I really going to be kicked out like this?"

I was reminded of the questions people had raised when I first started visiting North Korea. I had always maintained that helping the North Korean people was the right thing to do, even if my good efforts were repaid with evil. People were dying, and saving them was all that mattered.

North Korean officials had given no indication that they were even thinking of expelling me from their country. However, one of them did complain, "We're getting headaches from so many different people contacting us wanting to come in. Could you find a way to organize them together and designate one overall spokesperson we can deal with?"

"What do you mean?" I asked, as the realization of what had transpired came into focus. I had arranged for some people to visit

North Korea to pursue reunions with family members. These people apparently had independently contacted the North Korean authorities in attempts to set up their own operations inside the isolated country.

There had been no warnings, no friction, no animosity. Just a few days before, the North Korean officials had told me, "We fully trust you, Dr. Park, with all the medical work and help you've given us."

Then, suddenly, they excommunicated me and told me not to come at all.

One of the reasons, I thought, was due to the abrupt changes in the North Korean power structure. From the end of the 1980s to the mid-1990s, more reform-minded bureaucrats had been in charge. Given the closed and sequestered state of the North Korean society, the reforms were meager at best, but opened just enough to allow American medical personnel like myself to go in and work. However, in the late 1990s, those reformist bureaucrats were forced out by hard-line military officials, and the society as a whole became rigid and isolated once again.

Another reason, perhaps, was because I had become too much of a burden for the North Korean bureaucrats to bear. They had always been extremely uncomfortable with my uncompromising Christian faith and my persistence in mentioning Jesus whenever the opportunity allowed. The government's rigid opposition to Christianity, and, for that matter, any other form of organized religion, was well known. Lower-level bureaucrats worked under a scrutinizing cloud of incessant fear of reprisals from their superiors. I knew of instances where individuals helping North Koreans, such as myself, were suddenly detained under charges of espionage or "subversive activities via proselytizing" and imprisoned for months on end.

I quietly retreated, leaving without a complaint.

It was not until later that I found out that the true cause of my immediate banishment was the result of incriminating and accusatory words of those people I had helped to gain entrance to North Korea. Perhaps they envied my ministry or they wanted to establish their own. Whatever the reason, they surrendered to the North Korean authorities, recordings and printed documents of my testimonies shared in South Korea, the U.S., and around the world. I had gone through painstaking trouble to help these people obtain official cooperation from both the South Korean and North Korean governments necessary for their desired family reunions. And they returned the favor with outright betrayal. I was so sad to hear about these developments.

For the previous ten years I had trekked over many snow-capped mountains and through deep, hidden valleys in an isolated communist country where the remnants of the Cold War still lingered, for one purpose only—to save lives and souls. I had sacrificed myself, my career, my family, worldly comforts, possessions, and everything, only to find that the people I had trusted and helped had tried to destroy my ministry.

Oddly, I felt a strange sense of relief in what had happened. I was thankful that I would no longer have to go through the frustrating difficulties of mediating between North Korean officials and self-righteous sponsors who lacked understanding regarding the realities and true dangers of conducting mission and humanitarian work in North Korea. I also no longer would have to deal with the collusive North Korean officials. I had poured my life and energy into establishing and building the five-hundred-bed Pyong Yang Third Hospital, but I never once thought of it as mine. I had always known that a day would eventually come when the Lord would tell me to step down and walk away from this mission. I thought that this time had finally arrived.

I thanked the Lord for having allowed me the opportunity to serve Him in this capacity. Perhaps now, I could enjoy some peaceful rest. My work there had been fiercely difficult, and I had often wished for the opportunity to get myself out. My wish had come true, and I felt rather relieved.

Back home in America, my wife looked at me with a kind expression and said softly, "I truly respect you, Dear."

I looked up from my breakfast and stared at her blankly.

She continued, "Most people in your shoes wouldn't have kept quiet after what happened. They took away everything you worked so hard for. You sacrificed everything—career and time. We haven't even had a chance for a nice family get-together. Yet, you're not bitter or angry. You remain thankful, even though those ungrateful people in North Korea expelled you. For that, I truly respect you. You've demonstrated that your work was truly for the Lord and not merely to please men. I'm just so thankful that you're here, alive and well."

"What the Lord chooses to take away, I gladly surrender. But honey, I couldn't have done any of this work without your support and steadfast prayers and fasting for the ministry's sake. It was as much your work as it was mine," I responded.

We looked at each other for a brief moment as tears filled our eyes.

"As long as the Lord knows that we've followed Him with true hearts and minds, I'm content. We've no reason to hate or blame anyone. I actually feel rather grateful and relieved," I whispered.

"Since we're now freed from this mission, let's take some time for ourselves to travel, play golf, and enjoy reading as many books as we want. Let's have fun!" My wife's face eased into a smile as she wiped away her tears.

Despite our comforting words to each other, my heart remained unsettled. I pretended to be unbothered by my banishment, but deep down I was hurt and called fervently on the Lord for solace, direction, and purpose.

The troubles, in fact, did not end there. Once I was forbidden from entering North Korea, organizations I had been working with took turns in disowning me. In a sense, this instantaneous fall from veneration into scorned disfavor proved to be more hurtful to me than the North Korean banishment order itself. The Christian Association for Medical Missions (CAMM), an organization I had created and founded, excluded me from all of their activities. The United Korean Welfare Mission, another organization I had founded, moved to expel all non-Korean citizens from its organization, effectively banishing American passport-holders such as myself.

With ruthless efficiency, these two organizations of my own creation severed all their relations and ties with me. For the United Korean Welfare Mission alone, I had spent many years encouraging and persuading hundreds of thousands of individuals and churches to join its mission as sponsors. Now, I suddenly found myself completely alone without any support from people I had once considered close colleagues and friends.

"Since you've been placed on North Korea's blacklist and are forbidden from entering the country, we're going to have to ask you to remove yourself from any further association with the United Korean Welfare Mission. As a final farewell, we've taken up a private collection on your behalf," a board member said smugly, a man who in the past had many times accompanied me into North Korea. Amazingly, I had once considered him a friend. He placed a check in the amount of one million South Korean wons (about $1000) into my hand. I had to suppress the urge to tear up the check and throw the torn remnants into his face. Instead, gracefully, I resigned myself to accepting it.

These events reminded me all over again of a time when I had truly hated Korea and wished to forget about the country. In fact, when I had originally left after my graduation from medical school, I did so with the intention of *never* returning. Disappointment once again flooded my heart and mind, and I desperately desired some semblance of comfort and peace.

I felt lonelier each day.

"And we know that in all things God works for the good of those who love him, who have been called according to his purpose"
(Romans 8:28).

"Consider it pure joy, my brothers, whenever you face trials of many kinds, because you know that the testing of your faith develops perseverance" (James 1:2-3).

As One Door Closes, Another One Opens

All in all, I wished to recede quietly into a peaceful life and erase any thoughts of North Korea from my memory. But it was odd; I became busier as the days went by. I began receiving many invitations to share my testimony and North Korean mission experiences from across the country: Philadelphia, Houston, Washington DC. My days became inundated with speaking engagements. More and more people came to know about me through the print media and news broadcasts. Before long, I became a bit of a small-time celebrity. Sometimes when my wife and I would go out shopping, total strangers would approach.

"Aren't you Dr. Sai Park?"

"Uh . . . yes . . ."

"I was blessed when I read your column. I also saw you when you spoke at my church."

People began calling me at home for medical counseling. Others called for advice regarding their children. Some asked me to visit and pray for their sick loved ones. Many called to thank me.

When my wife and I had first moved to California from Michigan, one of the first people to befriend us was Pastor Hoon Bae, the lead pastor of the Korean Richmond Baptist Church in Richmond, California. Highly intrigued about my North Korean mission work, Pastor Bae asked me to come and speak to his congregation one Sunday afternoon. The response to my testimony was very enthusiastic, and a few months later my wife and I joined the church as regular members.

Pastor Bae began praying for North Korea and for my now defunct ministry, gently encouraging me to restart it. He introduced me to Jae Min Lee, an elder in the church who had a pressing burden in his heart for the North Korean people. Elder Lee and I, along with four other devout church members, began meeting each Saturday to collectively pray for North Korea. The more we sought the Lord's guidance, the more heightened our resolve became to restart the mission. These devout prayer partners insisted that we find God's will through my bitter past experiences. It was their prayers and encouragement that spurred me to even dare entertain thoughts about rekindling North Korean mission work again.

In November 1997, we founded the Christian Medical and Welfare Mission (CMWM). We began serious strategy discussions. Drawing from my past experiences of having worked primarily in Pyong Yang, the North Korean capital city—a city in which conditions were not as desperate as in the rest of the country—I was in favor of starting our new mission efforts in Najin Sunbong, a North Korean border city, a region specifically set apart by the government as a special economic free trade zone. There, foreigners were able to enter and exit with a bit more ease than anywhere else in North Korea.

My previous medical mission efforts in North Korea had centered only in Pyong Yang and had not reached the more wretched rural provinces throughout the country. I had once arranged for mobile hospital units to be sent to provide the rural areas with much needed medical care, but the North Korean authorities restricted the units to designated areas within Pyong Yang only. Additionally, we had built a noodle factory and sent instant noodles and medical supplies in several forty-foot shipping containers, but were never able to confirm how those products were distributed once they entered North Korea. The imposing scrutiny and suffocating constraints had effectively prevented my colleagues and I from treating or interacting directly with North Korean patients, which ran counter to our original intent.

My choice of Najin Sunbong was unanimously agreed on, and for CMWM's first mission project we launched a campaign called

"Sending Gifts of Love," which was sponsored by the *Korea Times* newspaper.

In May 1998, four months after the start of the campaign, eleven CMWM members and I set out for Najin Sunbong, North Korea. We had negotiated with the Economic Development Committee which governed the Najin Sunbong region. Therefore, we did not have to deal with the central government in Pyong Yang, and I was able to join them for the trip.

We decided to travel via an inland route through northeast China, crossing the Tumen River, which allowed us to completely bypass the North Korean authorities in Pyong Yang. I was still officially banned from ever entering North Korea.

Yet, by the Lord's amazing grace, and no small ironic coincidence, there I was, looking forward to traveling into North Korea once more and taking a new route into the country that had never before been utilized in my previous twenty trips into the country.

Amazing!

Sungsil

Days before my team and I left for Najin Sunbong, I received an urgent phone call. It was a missionary working in China who had been greatly supportive of my past mission work.

"Elder Park, I just learned of thirty North Korean refugees living in an underground shelter in Beijing. I was hoping that when you came to visit, you and your medical team could stop by to help."

"Is that true?"

"Yes, I've heard from a Korean-Chinese man who has been tending to them. He says the escapees are in really bad shape. They're suffering from extreme hypothermia. They have no warm clothes, no money, and there's nothing to eat."

"Yes, we'll definitely see them. If they've just come from North Korea, they're going to need a lot of help. Please arrange the meeting."

A few days later, another phone call came from the missionary.

"The North Korean refugees have been scattered. There was an argument among them that led to an accidental murder. The Chinese police came and arrested one of our Korean-Chinese helpers. The rest of them escaped to unknown places," said the missionary regretfully.

I felt so sorry and helpless.

A few days later my team and I arrived in Yonbian, China. We immediately met with the missionary colleague. He was anxious to fill me in on the news.

"Regarding the murder among the escapees, well, the murdered refugee had a thirteen-year-old daughter named Sungsil. After that whole fiasco she was brought here to Yonbian and sold to a slave trader. What can we do?" he asked.

"We have to save her! Put out an urgent search for her!" I instructed quickly. "Use whatever resources you have, but find the child!"

Within a few hours Sungsil was located, and we were able to buy her back from her slave trader. That night the twelve of us met Sungsil for the first time.

She had followed her father, risking her life to escape starvation and misery in North Korea, only to witness his murder. She was then sold as a slave before she had time to mourn her father's tragic death. We sat quietly, our hearts grieving for Sungsil. She seemed like a furious little beast. Her fear-stricken lips remained locked, and her fists were clenched tightly. She was unbelievably tiny for a thirteen-year-old girl; she could have easily passed for a child of eight or nine years of age. Clearly frightened, she was easily startled by the slightest touch or movement. Her large, bewildered eyes darted nervously back and forth. That night the twelve of us appealed to the Lord with fervent prayers on her behalf.

As I embraced the traumatized child, I began to gain a clearer understanding of the harrowing plight of the North Korean refugees.

"Let's help Sungsil in any way possible. We must help the refugees," I whispered to my colleagues.

Suddenly, Sungsil sank limply to the floor and burst out into a loud, anguished, wailing sob. She was inconsolable. Tearfully, we continued to pray for the Holy Spirit's peace, love, and healing. Afterward, we emptied our wallets of all the money in our possession and collected more than $4,500 that night. After much discussion, we decided that it would be best to entrust her in the care of a kind Korean-Chinese female deacon I knew and trusted in Harbin, China. Sungsil was sent to Harbin the very next day.

As we continued on our way to Najin Sunbong, we came to the Tumen River, one of the two rivers on the border between North Korea and China. We were inundated with many tragic stories of North Korean refugees crossing the river in desperate search of food and survival. Some had relatives in China and were able to obtain food for their families back home, but most were not so fortunate. Most refugees were helpless. For these people, there was no one to turn to and nowhere to go. There was no relief to be found in China. Due to the political reciprocities between the two neighboring communist nations, it was illegal and highly dangerous to be a North Korean refugee in China, and it was illegal for anyone to help them. Many North Korean women stealthily crossed the river at night to sell their bodies in exchange for food, to feed starving children waiting back home. My heart broke upon hearing this news.

It was a bright spring morning and the sky was a clear pale blue. My team and I stood on the banks of the sunlit Tumen River, holding hands to pray. We watched as the sparkling water swirled mirthfully by, carefree, as if all was well in the world and nothing tragic had ever happened here. As a nation, Korea had suffered throughout its tumultuous history from countless foreign invasions and brutally oppressive occupations. My ancestors would have shed blood and tears on this very river.

And today, many of our North Korean brethren were risking—and losing—their lives here as well. These people are so desperate to survive. The river looks so serene, but when will we be able to look upon this place without tragedy and sadness? I asked myself. My heart grieved.

Together we wept and prayed, calling on the mercy of our Lord Jesus Christ.

Najin Sunbong

Najin Sunbong Hospital was nothing more than a four-hundred-fifty bed, run down, old building. The conditions in this hospital proved to be as sparse and inadequate as the hospitals in Pyong Yang. Most of the medical equipment and supplies looked antiquated and nonfunctional. The hospital possessed no medicines, not even simple pain killers. My team and I had brought some $200,000 worth of medicine and medical supplies with us from the U.S. As we began unloading and unpacking the large supply boxes, looks of awe came over the faces of the hospital staff watching. I was thrilled to see how happy this made them.

One member of our team was a reporter from the *Korea Times Newspaper*. Although she dared not reveal her true occupation to the North Korean officials—as it was illegal to travel into North Korea with members of the press—undeterred, the *Korea Times* had sent her. The newspaper was a major sponsor of our campaign, and we didn't think twice about undertaking the risk of having her join us. She meticulously documented our activities by taking thousands of photographs. Her actions aroused the suspicions of the Najin Sunbong officials, and they began probing me with pointed questions, "What does she do for a living?" I did my best to answer without divulging too much.

However, one particular afternoon, I got carried away and inadvertently revealed her identity. "Reporter Chung, hurry and take a picture of this," I instructed, pointing to some of the boxes of medicine and equipment we had brought with us.

Immediately, a stern looking North Korean official pulled me aside and hissed, "You brought in a reporter with you. I knew it! You'd better make sure that you keep quiet about this! Do you hear me?"

We were thankful that the official did not make an issue of it. As nervous as we were for having been caught with a reporter on our team, our North Korean guides were now extremely fearful for having accidentally allowed a reporter into the country.

While in Najin Sunbong, I was scheduled to perform hysterectomies on two patients. Surveying the capacity of the operating room the night before left me feeling anxious and panicked. The operating room more closely resembled an old barn than it did a surgical area. My team and I had prepared specialized tools and medical supplies from the U.S., assuming that the most basic medical and surgical equipment would be available. However, there was nothing. There was not even simple equipment for administering anesthesia.

How would I get oxygen or blood in the event of an emergency? Surgical operations under such conditions could lead to dangerous complications. My mind was filled with apprehension, and I prayed throughout the night. "Dear Lord, you know that it'll be impossible for me to perform major surgery under these conditions. If one of these patients dies, our mission will be in jeopardy and we'll all be finished."

I could hear no answer and increasingly agonized as to how to proceed. What do you want me to do, Lord?

When I woke the next morning, the Lord made His answer clearly evident. The hotel was completely blacked out. No electricity. But it was not just the hotel; the entire city that day was blacked out. The North Korean officials looked terribly embarrassed. The hospital staff milled around frantically as they tried in vain to restore power with weak generators.

The surgeries could not be performed. The Lord was making it known that He was not only protecting His mission, He was leading it! Hallelujah! The two patients of the aborted surgeries continued to beseech me. I still remember the tearful plea of one of the women as she begged, "Dear doctor, please save me. I can't stand the pain any longer."

Although the operations could not take place, I arranged for the president of the Najin Sunbong Hospital to send them to a hospital in a nearby province, the Chungjin Provincial Hospital, for their surgeries.

Though my team and I were granted access to treat and interact directly with patients in Najin Sunbong, the restrictions in this area did not turn out to be any lighter than in Pyong Yang. In fact, the ever-present scrutiny and limiting controls were equally excessive. Accomplishing any work in Najin Sunbong required obtaining consent not only from the authorities there, but also from government officials in Pyong Yang!

Additionally, due to the more open economic policies in this region, overall living conditions in Najin Sunbong were less dire. This area was better off than most provinces in North Korea. We felt that this necessitated a redirection of our attention to areas where there was more urgent need for our assistance.

After much deliberation, we concluded that Najin Sunbong was not to be the area of focus for our mission. We asked the Lord to show us where to place our concentration instead and began to think of either Wonsan or Sin Eu Ju as possible alternatives.

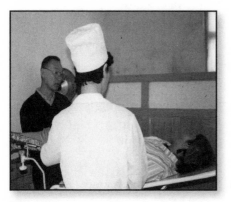

Treating patients at Najin Sunbong Hospital

The Spring of Life

"Is the Christian Medical and Welfare Mission an organization that only medical personnel can participate in? Is there a way for people other than medical practitioners to join?" I was once asked this question in a television interview.

"Of course," I responded. "Participation in CMWM is open to everyone—medical professionals and laymen. Anyone can partner with us through active participation on the mission field, financial support, or prayers."

That interview prompted me to rethink the focus of our mission. Medicine was a means, a tool, for our mission, but certainly not our goal. Our ultimate objective was to save souls. If we were going to turn our organization into an effective soul-saving engine for the Lord, it was incumbent upon us to first awaken and prepare ourselves spiritually. In keeping with our redirected purpose, we decided to rename our organization.

But what name would best describe our mission? I searched for the answer in my prayers. Inspiration came to me one morning, as I was praising the Lord with my favorite hymn, "Come All Ye Who Are Thirsty."

Come, ye disconsolate, where'er ye languish
Come to the mercy seat, fervently kneel
Here bring your wounded hearts, here tell your anguish
Earth has no sorrow that heav'n cannot heal.
Joy of the desolate, light of the straying
Hope of the penitent, fadeless and pure
Here speaks the Comforter, tenderly saying
Earth has no sorrow that heav'n cannot cure.

All who draw nigh and take, here, of God's bounty
Shall know a spring of Life, still to increase
Water of life shall flow up from within them

Ending all thirsting and never to cease.

My heart was suddenly gripped by the word *sam*. In the Korean text the words *spring water* are composed of Korean characters phonetically pronounced as *sam*. I immediately connected the word *sam* to the hymn's words "spring of Life." Yes! We'll call our organization SAM, the Spiritual Awakening Mission, and awaken souls with the thirst quenching water from the spring of Life, our Lord Jesus Christ.

"O Lord, thank you! Don't ever let me stray. May my spirit stay awakened and sensitive to your promptings and voice forever," I whispered through my tears.

My wife brought a cup of tea to my study and saw me overcome with emotion. "What happened?" she asked alarmed.

I shared with her how the Lord had blessed me in my early morning prayers and led me to the word *sam*. Together, we sang praises of joy.

Sam is a familiar and easy word to remember in both the Korean and English languages. It is an abbreviated version of the name Samuel. The U.S. government is sometimes referred to as Uncle Sam. Everyone seemed pleased with the name.

We changed the name of our mission from CMWM to SAM and chose Sin Eu Ju, North Korea, as the new target of our focus. After much strategizing, tentative plans were drawn to establish a presence in Sin Eu Ju, which could potentially function as our base inside of North Korea. Lengthy negotiations with North Korean officials ensued. On October 25, 1998, together with officials from Sin Eu Ju, we signed a final Memorandum of Understanding (MOU). SAM was now considered to be a sister organization to the Sin Eu Ju Provincial Hospital. We would assist by furnishing medical supplies, equipment, machinery, and medicines. Daunting though the task would surely be, I had every confidence that the Lord would faithfully fulfill what He had initiated.

I immediately mobilized a SAM team of doctors and arranged for their deployment into Sin Eu Ju. However, two weeks before the team's departure date, the North Korean government abruptly nullified everything. They arrested and jailed our Korean-Chinese liaison for five weeks. He had gone ahead into Sin Eu Ju to finalize arrangements for our team's stay.

The reason was simple. The rise of hardliners within the North Korean hierarchy meant dissipating tolerance toward Christian organizations such as ours. Furthermore, as South Korean big business conglomerates began pouring millions of dollars into North Korea, our relatively small-scale contributions must have seemed petty in their view. For very little money (from their perspective), we had too many conditions and demands about worshiping God and treating patients ourselves.

"We'll postpone the visit by one year," they told us bluntly.

We protested. "Why do you postpone what has already been agreed to and planned?"

"The visit has to be postponed by a year." It was a unilateral decision, and we had no say in the matter. Our entire plan had suddenly gone bust.

We needed a change in strategy. If my past dealings and experiences with the North Korean government were any indication, our work would always be undermined at their slightest whim, unless we sought a way around the incessant volatility and the plaguing unpredictability.

I recalled reports I had read a while ago regarding the desperate life and death plight of North Korean refugees along the river banks. "How about changing our plans and embarking on a vision trip along the Tumen and Yalu Rivers instead?" I suggested to the team members.

Everyone agreed. We decided to undertake a 3,000-li (750 miles) trek along the Tumen and Yalu River banks to see, hear, help, and pray.

"God will open a new mission during our journey."

"God will lead our path."

With that, we soothed our disappointment regarding the aborted Sin Eu Ju mission.

The Vision Trip along the Tumen and Yalu Rivers

July 1999. Our team of four doctors, two dentists, two nurses, and four non-medical volunteers left for a twelve-day, 750-mile vision trip. We would be traveling through such places as Russia; Hunchoon, China; and Jang Baek, China.

Our first destination was Ussrisk, Russia, near Vladivostok. We met Mary, a middle-aged Korean-Russian woman, who was a native Russian speaker with fluency in the Korean language. She served as our translator. She was deeply moved by our mission efforts and devoted herself to tirelessly assisting us during our stay.

"Many Koreans came here during the Chosun Dynasty one hundred years ago in search of food. As the number of them grew, the Soviet Union forcefully deported them (about 100,000 people) by train to Uzbekistan and Kazhakstan, central regions within the Soviet Union. On those trains one third of the people froze to death and another third starved to death. Only a small number of them survived. Today those Korean-Russians are known as the Kareskii. The Kareskii minorities have suffered great discrimination." She pointed to a group of people standing on the street corner, dressed in flimsy, tattered clothing. They were huddled together in attempts to keep warm from the icy winds. "They are the Kareskii people," she said.

Many of the Kareskii lived in run-down detention camps. The old barracks were greatly dilapidated, filthy, and infested with rats. We had brought bags of rice with us and distributed as many as possible. People became tearful with gratitude as they accepted the grains.

Pointing to a train running across the vast plains around Ussrisk, Mary said, "Those trains run regularly from Wonsan, North Korea, to Moscow via this plain. Many North Koreans come here in search of relief from their suffering and starvation. But the situation here is dire, too. These people don't have homes and wander the streets in search of food. Only some of them can speak Russian. The situation is very urgent. We need to provide these people with basic living necessities. These people need Jesus in their lives."

I listened to Mary speaking of the plight of our Korean-Russian brethren here in Ussrisk and let out a deep sigh. What a place! Just three hundred fifty miles away from the South Korean border, and, yet, here was another disaster about which the world community was oblivious.

We set up a makeshift clinic and tacked on a free medical care sign on the front. Within minutes, we were inundated with hundreds of patients eagerly flocking around us. Our doctors and nurses carefully tended to each person's illness and ailments. Our non-medical volunteers strived diligently to keep order around the mini-clinic, keeping patients company as they waited to be seen by the doctors and gently guiding people from station to station.

As patients made their way toward the exit, our team pastor embraced and prayed with many. People broke down into tears of appreciation and gratitude for strangers from a faraway land who had come to help them, serve them, and lavish them with love. The patients were encouraged not to thank us, but to instead say, "Hallelujah!" and "Amen!"

Many of the patients turned out to be Korean-Russians, with a few having come from North Korea. "Me? It's been some time since I first started working here as a timber logger. But there are too many of us. I came in the hopes of a better life, but it's not any better here than it is back home. I guess that's just how it is with life," a laborer from North Korea said as he shrugged. His weathered, worn hands and rugged knuckles were peppered with jagged scars—some old, some new. Each scar seemed to speak volumes of a lifetime of bitter hardships.

As I treated patients throughout the day, I learned more about the harsh realities for North Koreans in Ussrisk. Many tried futilely to obtain work as timber loggers. People arrived with great anticipation and hopes of making money. Yet life remained miserable and wretched. Travel by train from North Korea to Ussrisk should normally take no more than three days. But with frequent delays and mechanical breakdowns, these trips usually ended up taking five to six days instead. In extreme temperatures of hot or cold weather, these journeys became deadly. North Koreans would begin their trip with only a few rice rolls, and, by the end, many were half-dead from starvation or diarrhea from eating food that had become spoiled along the way.

Many of these people journeyed from North Korea without socks or shoes; a great majority of them suffered frostbite well before the onset of the winter season. People were severely malnourished, with no access to food, doctors, medicine, or shelter. Relatively minor conditions escalated into catastrophic, life-threatening illnesses.

On our final day in Ussrisk, we arranged a worship service at a local high school auditorium. With approximately one thousand people in attendance, I preached in Korean, and Mary stood beside me, translating into Russian. As the service progressed, we lifted our voices together in mighty praise to the Holy One. The entire auditorium became beautifully diffused with the sweet presence of His Holy Spirit.

I watched in amazement as hundreds of these attendees unhesitatingly came forward, flowing in from all sides of the auditorium, to receive Jesus Christ as their personal Savior for the very first time. They were so desperate for hope, for a Savior. As a great burden burgeoned inside me to bring the gospel to this land of tremendous thirst and need, a new vision sprang to my mind. In becoming disciples of the Lord, these people would be able to share the Good News throughout all of Russia and Asia. Perhaps, He was specially preparing them for those specific regions of the world! They already knew the language, geography, and culture.

"This is what God intends for these people!" I cheered triumphantly.

Korea is only a small peninsula nation, but, proximity-wise, it is surrounded by great, dominating powers of Northeast Asia. It remains divided, the only such nation on earth, bordered by countries that brutally persecute Christians. Still, the Lord's will is alive and well in those regions.

This is His great secret.

Worship service at Ussrisk, Russia

Our Vision

We started each morning at 6:00 a.m., with quiet time and prayer. Though our days were long and full, and we were physically spent and exhausted, no one complained.

We did not anticipate how strongly we would bond with the people of Ussrisk until we were about to leave. Mary could not bear to part with us there and opted to follow us along the tough one-day journey back to the Russian-Chinese border. "Please remember us and please promise to come back. This is goodbye for now, but it's my hope that we'll see each other again very soon," Mary said as she hugged us.

As we waved goodbye, I thought to myself, We've got to come back here. We've got to open a clinic and have a full-time missionary stay with these people to share the hope of the gospel.

We headed to our next destination on an old Chinese bus, which sped along a dirt road just adjacent to the Tumen River. I glanced casually out the window as the North Korean countryside blurred by, when a strange image caught the corner of my eye. I immediately sat up, turned my head to look more closely and gasped. Floating in the water along the North Korean shore was a corpse partially stuck to a large rock. The body was a strange bluish hue and looked shockingly swollen. No one would have been able to identify the person.

Why was the corpse lying there? Why did he have to die? People were forced to risk their lives just to survive, just to exist. Of all the years I had been coming to North Korea to save lives, had my efforts been in vain? Had I been of any help at all? It seemed as if the corpse was shouting to me about the inadequacies of my work.

I was then reminded of an incident that had happened a few years before. A phone call came to me from a pastor in South Korea. His church wanted to send pediatric medicine to save North Korean children—a full shipping container.

"Sending the medicine can be arranged with no problem. However, once it enters North Korean borders, no one knows exactly what happens to those goods, how they're distributed or utilized," I explained.

"I understand, but we still want to send them. North Korean children are dying in the thousands from smallpox, measles, and diarrhea. We want to send the medicine, no matter what. Even if we save just one child, it's worth it. Please help us do this," the pastor insisted.

"Yes, of course. We'll prepare the medications."

The church raised the funds, and we duly informed the North Korean government of our intent to send one forty-foot shipping container of children's medications, with a possible market value of up to $1,000,000. We worked with a U.S. pharmaceutical company in preparing the container. The final bill came to a market value of $690,000, based on a heavily discounted price. We sent the container as it was.

Some time later, a call came to me from North Korea. "You said you would ship us $1,000,000 worth of medicines, so how come you sent us only $690,000 worth?" a North Korean official asked suspiciously.

"We promised to send you one forty-foot container full of medicines with a possible market value of up to $1,000,000," I explained incredulously. "The drugs that were sent to you are of top quality. They're not expired or left-over medications. Please accept them and put them to good use so that the lives of thousands of your children will be saved."

"You promised us $1,000,000 worth of medicines. Therefore, we're expecting you to send us $1,000,000 worth!" the North Korean official demanded.

Flabbergasted, words failed me at that moment. I did not even know how I should respond.

"You Christians are liars!" the official sneered accusingly.

It was pointless to even attempt an explanation. In the end, we sent an additional twenty-foot container full of medicine.

According to the United Nations, North Korea frequently sells off medicines received from international organizations to other nations in order to buy oil and sells food donations in exchange for hard currency. Of course, the North Korean government vehemently denies any such actions.

When I first started my North Korean ministry, I put forth my best efforts with the earnest belief that our unconditional love and sincerest endeavors to save lives would soften hardened hearts and soothe broken spirits. Experiencing these kinds of questionable incidents was slowly corroding our unwavering commitment, supplanting our good will with darkened doubt and disillusionment. Had our efforts only served to buttress the North Korean government's stronghold and dominance over its people? Had the consequences of our mission been, in actuality, a perpetuation and prolonging of the people's suffering, rather than an alleviation of them?

Being confronted with the corpse strengthened my resolve.

"Yes, the river banks are where we must carry out our mission!" I shouted defiantly at that moment.

"During the night, Paul had a vision of a man of Macedonia standing and begging him, 'Come over to Macedonia and help us'" (Acts 16: 9).

Much like the Macedonian man in Paul's vision, I felt as if the corpse was calling out to us for help. Perhaps this was why the Lord had pushed me out of North Korea and led me to this river bank! Transporting containers of aid to North Korea, in and of itself, was meaningless for the actual suffering masses there. However, if people could find the courage and fortitude to somehow make their way to the treacherous Chinese border, we could directly interact with them, feed them, heal them, care for them, and instill in them an inextinguishable hope, the love of Christ. Perhaps, they would then choose to live as His disciples upon their return to North Korea and minister messages of His love and hope to their families, friends, neighbors, and, eventually, the entire nation.

Thank you, Lord, for giving us a new vision. Thank you for leading the way.

Jesus Is the Captain

Following the Lord's prompting, my SAM medical team and I left for our third 750-mile medical mission journey along the Tumen and Yalu Rivers. One of our primary challenges was the safe passage of our enormous supplies of medicine and equipment through customs at the Russian-Chinese border. There were six large boxes including a mobile dental unit.

Both Russia and China prohibited such items from entering their borders from abroad. Our prior attempts to obtain official and legal approval through various channels had failed. Among our personal belongings, we had hidden as many of the medicines as we could carry, just as we had done during our first two trips along this same route. If caught, our medical supplies and equipment would have been confiscated and we would have been punished to the fullest extent of the law, according to each country. We prayed desperately for safe passage.

As we had feared and somewhat anticipated, the Russian customs agents were very suspicious, especially of the odd looking dental instruments and equipment. Today we have far less trouble with Russian and Chinese customs agents, as many of them are now sympathetic to our medical mission work. However, this was not the case at that particular time.

"We're bringing this medicine and equipment to help the Russian people, to help your people. And we'll take it back with us when we leave," we pleaded. It was no use. We were caught, and they were not going to allow us to simply pass through.

The agents scrutinized the dental equipment closely and seemed to hesitate. Apparently, they had no notion as to how to proceed and which laws applied in this particular circumstance. None of them had ever seen such strange contraptions before. We waited anxiously as they proceeded to alert their superiors of the befuddling situation.

Twenty minutes passed, then forty. In the meantime, all the other travelers had left the airport, and everything stilled to a hushed quiet. The customs officers continued to detain our dentist, Dr. Lim, and the dental equipment. Their concentrated focus on the dental equipment only, had caused their neglect in checking the contents of the additional six boxes with us, which allowed the rest of our group to easily pass through.

Two hours later, our dental equipment and dentist were still being held. We prepared for a worst-case scenario and were ready to relinquish the dental equipment; we could see no other resolution. To our great surprise, they eventually allowed both Dr. Lim and the dental equipment to pass through. They could not find anyone who knew anything about such equipment, and their superiors had been equally baffled as well.

"Ah! The Lord walks with us. He's in control!" we exclaimed excitedly as we finally made our way toward the airport exit.

We made a return visit to the city of Ussrisk, and our first stop was an old Russian auditorium that had been set up for a SAM revival conference. From the outside, the jubilant sounds of hymns and praises floated in the air. About one thousand Russians were gathered, singing praises, and responding with hearty amens and hallelujahs. The giant placard at the front of the auditorium read, "SAM Russia Conference—1999."

I made my way to the podium and addressed the audience. "I excitedly anticipate the day when Russians will traverse to the ends of the earth as Christian missionaries for the entire world!"

I spoke to the audience in English. Mary, our translator from our previous visit, stood beside me, translating my sermon into Russian. The congregation nodded their heads in agreement to my message and shouted enthusiastic amens.

The following day, we set up a makeshift clinic and provided free medical care to many Russian citizens in Ussrisk. We also spent time offering discipleship training to the local volunteers—Korean-Russians and Korean-Chinese—who had been active in assisting North Korean escapees along the Tumen and Yalu Rivers. Open discussions were conducted as to how best to carry out North Korean missions in this region.

To our great delight, twenty local doctors stepped forward and made the commitment to volunteer their time and services to our mission. Their participation enabled us to set up a small clinic in Ussrisk, the first of what would eventually become many. "I feel like I'm dreaming," Mary said happily. We hired a local doctor and a nurse to oversee the clinic activities on a full-time basis and left them with many of the medicine and medical supplies we had laboriously brought with us.

Vladivostok was our next destination where we conducted more free medical clinics. After three nights and four days of medical services there, we crossed the Russian Yunhae Province and arrived at a guard station near the Russian-Chinese border around three o'clock in the afternoon. From that point on, only designated vehicles could cross the border into China.

We waited for the daily bus that would take us into Hunchoon, China, but the bus scheduled for a five o'clock pick up never arrived. We asked the guards about this and were told that the bus to Hunchoon would run only if passengers were present from the start of the bus route. If there were no riders, the bus would not come. The guard station closed at six, and, if by that time it had not arrived, we would be forced to spend the night in the open field.

It was 6:10 p.m. We were dead tired and sleep deprived. Arranging our luggage in a pile, we hunkered down for an apprehensive wait. Ten minutes passed, fifteen, twenty. Finally, a vehicle could be seen approaching in the distance. It was a bus with fifty Chinese people returning from a day trip into Russia. This was not the Hunchoon bus for which we had been waiting; but, when we explained our predicament to the driver, he kindly let us aboard.

The bus took us through a Russian customs checkpoint. The officials at this location were notorious for their meticulous and methodical inspection of passengers' belongings. We prayed for quick and safe passage and the Lord answered with the covering of His protection. The customs agents allowed us to pass through without so much as a second glance at our bulky luggage, stating that it was late already. To our amazement, we breezed through what was reputed to be one of the toughest customs check points without the loss of even a single aspirin. Thank you, Lord!

It was 7:00 p.m. We arrived at a Chinese customs checkpoint, another tough hurdle. At that hour, the customs office had already closed for the evening. We were forced to wait two long hours in the neutral zone between the borders until the office reopened.

When the Chinese customs agent arrived, he began hurriedly checking the luggage of the Chinese tourists first; we waited toward the end of the line. Having been called in for an impromptu late shift, the agent was irritable and sped through the motions of perfunctory inspections, at best.

When it was our turn, he glanced at us casually and asked if we had any illegal items in our luggage. We responded in the negative, and he quickly passed us through with a dismissive wave of his hand. It was nothing short of a miracle the way the Lord had navigated us through these tough customs inspection checkpoints with such ease.

The remainder of the medicine and equipment we had brought with us were put to good use in treating hundreds of patients in China. With each clinic, patients flocked eagerly around us in a rush to be treated first. Often we did not even have time to put on our masks or latex gloves. With bare hands, we tenderly cared for our patients, treating their wounds and illnesses. We did our utmost to comfort and encourage the sick, the weak, the downtrodden. With tears flowing and arms interlocked in loving embraces, I do not know who was more blessed, we or they.

Over the Mountains, Through the Deep Valley

We had left Yonbion, China, at 8:00 a.m. and did not arrive at Jang Baek, China, until 11:00 p.m. The road conditions were horrible, with most of the roads pockmarked and jagged. Around 3:00

p.m. the bus broke down along a rugged mountainside road. The oil filter had ruptured, causing the engine oil to leak profusely. The driver left us in the bus on the side of the road and quickly ambled down to a nearby village in search of alternative transportation.

With the dental tools we had brought with us, we tried to fix the broken oil filter ourselves. But being doctors and not mechanics, we probably did more damage than good. The air was stiflingly hot and humid, with giant mosquitoes buzzing incessantly. To the west, the sun was beginning to set early along the mountainside road, but none of us dared to turn on the lights for fear of attracting some unknown beast from the depths of the shadowy trees. Yet no one complained. We were filled with the joy of the Holy Spirit and passed the time praying and singing praises.

At 5:00 p.m. we noticed the backlights of a large vehicle quickly approaching; a bus was being driven in reverse toward us. It was the bus driver who had gone for help. Because the road was too narrow to make a U-turn at any point, he had driven the bus in reverse for more than an hour to pick us up.

"Wow!" we shouted simultaneously. Gratefully, we boarded. As our bus bucked and surged along the bumpy roads, a colleague in the seat behind me began singing a hymn and we all heartily joined in.

Walking in sunlight all of my journey
Over the mountains, through the deep valley
Jesus has said, "I'll never forsake thee"
Promise divine that never can fail.

Overwhelmed by the beauty of the words, we choked back rising tears.

After three or more hours of riding along a steep mountainous road, the bus abruptly came to a standstill. Though the bus driver was an experienced local operator, he had made a wrong turn somewhere down the mountain and strayed into a dead end in the dark. On the serpentine, single-lane cliff road, in the dead of night, the driver had to make his way painstakingly back down the mountain, driving in reverse, as the road was still too narrow to make a U-turn anywhere. My heart quickened as I nervously prayed, "Oh Jesus! Please be with us, especially the driver. If we fall off this road, that'll be the end of us!"

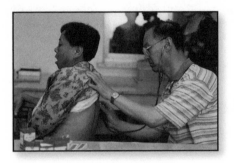

As the bus rolled backwards, twisting and turning for more than three hours, I kept my eyes closed and fervidly called on the name of the Lord. And, we made it. We finally arrived at Jang Baek.

Treating patients at border clinic

Sungchan

We became connected to a small underground church situated along the Tumen River in Jang Baek. They sought out our help in assisting North Korean refugees who had escaped in search of food and medicine. During one of our visits, the pastor asked us to treat a sick North Korean child refugee under their care. The boy was small and extremely emaciated. His head was abnormally large for his tiny body. He looked to be no more than ten years old. His name was Sungchan.

"The boy is seventeen years old," the pastor informed us.

With stunned disbelief, we carefully examined him. He was in a state of extreme malnutrition, and his severely underdeveloped physique indicated a delay in the onset of puberty. The youth would have starved to death without the church's intervention. We gave Sungchan intravenous fluids to address his dehydration and fed him enriched nutritional supplements. We left him with all the money in our possession.

Later that week, one of my colleagues arrived at the church with a woman eight months pregnant. "A Chinese man was dragging her by the hair, trying to force her onto a train," he explained. "She was screaming. So I ran over to them and asked the man what he was doing; he told me that he had bought her as a slave. I had to stop him, so I bought back her freedom!"

He was able to negotiate a price of 200 yuan (about $25) to buy the woman out of slavery. Her story was tragic: "It was difficult to live in the mountains. I couldn't go back to North Korea either. While I wandered along the Tumen River, I was caught and sold to the Chinese man."

One month later, this woman gave birth to a son in the home of one of the underground Korean-Chinese deacons. We named the child Joo Il Saeng, meaning "dedicated to the Lord." For some time, she and her son remained hidden in the basement of that underground church. During our time with her, we shared the gospel with her and gave her a small Bible to read. Eventually, she came to accept Jesus as her Savior and dedicated her life to God. Not long ago, I received the following letter—

Dear Doctor:

While my own parents deserted me, our Heavenly Father has given me new life and hope. He has blessed me with His safety and security. For this amazing grace, I'm in tears everyday, thanking my Heavenly Father. I commit myself to studying the Bible to help save my people in North Korea. I'd like to express my deepest thanks to you for keeping me in this safe and warm place where I'm learning about the amazing love of our God.

In Jang Baek, there were many farm villages with third- and fourth-generation Korean-Chinese families (about eighty to a hundred households per village), located deep in the forests. Due to a lack of health care, many of these families suffered chronic diseases: advanced tuberculosis, debilitating arthritis, high blood pressure, and liver maladies. We set up free medical clinics and treated as many people as possible.

Astonishingly, some North Korean refugees were able to find their way to our clinics in desperate search of food. We provided them everything we could: food, clothes, medications, Bibles. They were all receptive to receiving prayer.

It is my hope that these people will someday rise to become soldiers in God's heavenly army, spiritual warriors through which the Lord's mighty message of love and salvation will break through that frozen land encapsulated in an icy veil of darkness. In the meantime, the arduous task of pursuing North Korean missions must go forward.

Dan Dong

After four days of conducting medical missions in Jang Baek, our plan was to travel along the banks of the Yalu River to get as close to Sin Eu Ju, North Korea, as possible. We braced ourselves for another long bus journey. Unfortunately, mechanical problems persistently plagued our bus. Our plans to leave at six o'clock in the morning after an early prayer service were hampered by a two hour delay due to tire problems.

While we waited for the tire to be fixed, I noticed a vendor roasting chestnuts nearby. No one had bought any, and he had kept them roasting on a fire for hours. His chestnuts looked more like little black pebbles. I bought a large bag and brought the charred nuts onto the bus with me. Not surprisingly, no one wanted any.

We had been riding for several hours, speeding along the unpaved, bumpy road as the bus violently jolted and jerked like a wild horse. "Dr. Park, will our internal organs remain in the same place after this ride?" someone joked.

It seems so funny now, but our cross-country, mountain-trekking bus rides back then were nothing short of perilous and unpredictable. The roads we traveled along were unpaved and sometimes would suddenly disappear, and without warning we would find ourselves crashing into a stream. One time the road suddenly disappeared and the bus plowed headlong into a farmer's mountainous pile of animal manure.

Our Chinese bus broke down easily and seemed especially prone to incessant oil leaks. It seems so silly now when I think of all the times we tried, in vain, to use our dental tools to fix the mechanical problems underneath the bus. All in all, I think we pushed the bus more than we rode in it.

There were times when I wondered whether I would ever make it out of the mountains alive in time to meet my first grandchild who was due to make his grand entrance into the world any day.

Poor driver—he was a real champ. His tireless energy and seemingly superhuman ability to expertly maneuver the bus, forward or backwards, day or night, never ceased to amaze us.

It was 7:00 p.m. We had skipped all three meals as there was no place to obtain food along the endlessly bumpy road. Famished and weary, none of us could muster strength to even move.

"Dr. Park what about those roasted chestnuts you bought?" someone said. We shared the chestnuts in the dark, rattling bus, not able to see if the pieces we were eating were burned or rotten. Even so, we managed to stave off our hunger with those wonderfully charred little nuts!

"God is so good. God is so good. God is so good to me."

Someone sang the words, his voice choking with rising emotion. Unable to continue, the person sitting next to him picked up the song. Soon we were all singing and in tears. "Yes, our God is so good. He is so good."

This mission team was an extraordinary compilation of men. Each had a busy life with a successful, respected, career. It made very little sense that we would feel such joy and gratitude for the provision of a couple of burned chestnuts, enjoyed deep in the heart of remote mountains, far removed from the amenities of our comfortable lives back home. Yet, we were elated.

> It was heaven on earth.
> God fills our stomach even if we don't eat!
> God keeps us fresh even if we don't rest!
> I thought I had to eat to be full,
> Sleep to feel rested,
> Own a house to feel secure,
> But I was wrong.
> One doesn't need food to feel full,
> Nor water to quench one's thirst.
> If the Lord is with us,
> As long as our good God is with us.

We drove continuously through the night and as the awakening dawn broke through the black sky, a cell phone rattled. "Hey, we're back in touch with the outside world again," someone said sleepily. "We've made it!"

The colleague who answered the cell phone suddenly turned around, his face exploded into a huge grin and he boomed, "Elder Park, you've become a grandfather. Your daughter, Bette, has given birth to a son!"

The bus erupted into a great round of applause. The news brought infinite joy and a great jolt of courage to us all.

"I'm a grandfather!" I exclaimed happily. I was thoroughly enthralled and could not remember ever being so excited. When my wife had given birth to our children, I was always too busy or preoccupied to appropriately cherish those miraculous events. But, with the news of my grandson's birth, I wanted to leap for joy.

The Lord interjected in each of us a sense of renewed hope and encouragement through the news. We all felt strengthened as if each of us had become grandfathers that day.

It had been twenty-six hours since we had left Jang Baek. We ignored the growling protestations of our empty stomachs and asked the driver, "Where are we?"

"Dan Dong," he answered.

No one had heard of Dan Dong, China, but we felt that the Holy Spirit had specifically led us there. We got off the bus and worshiped the Lord, praying, "Thank you, Lord, for leading us safely to this place through our hunger and our travels through rough and dangerous terrains."

Much to our surprise, we learned that Dan Dong, China, was exactly one mile directly across the Yalu River from Sin Eu Ju, North Korea! We marveled at the way in which the Lord had directed us precisely there to make Dan Dong one of the outposts of our mission. It seemed as if He was telling us, "Don't let the North Korean authorities push you around anymore. Help those who flee from North Korea, here, at Dan Dong. Impart my message of love and hope. Teach them about me!"

We resolved to set up a hospital there.

We carried the bus more than it carried us

7

The Dan Dong-CMWM Hospital

I was introduced to the Dan Dong City Health Department officials through a SAM colleague who had business dealings in China.

"I'm an American," I said to the officials at our initial meeting. "I'd like to build a hospital in Dan Dong." The Chinese officials were enthusiastically receptive to the idea. My colleagues and I were taken to an empty, run-down building located some distance from the bustling downtown area. Though we were not familiar with Dan Dong City, we could sense that the Chinese officials were attempting to pass off a worthless building to us. As our purpose for the hospital was to treat not only Chinese locals but also North Korean refugees, the quiet, slightly-out-of-the-way location seemed well suited to our needs. It was highly illegal to be associated with North Korean refugees in any manner. Also, I felt a sense of assurance in my spirit that the Lord had led us to this building. We accepted the offer.

February 1999. An agreement was established between the city of Dan Dong and SAM International to run a hospital under joint American-Chinese ownership. The "joint ownership" was in name only. The city of Dan Dong would provide the run-down building, but we were expected to fully renovate and equip the hospital with everything necessary for it to become completely operational. The task before us was daunting. As I had only recently become free of the assaulting burden of building the Pyong Yang Third Hospital, the thought of beginning another behemoth hospital project felt burdensome.

The hospital was to be renovated in a lodging style so that the facility could function both as a medical hospital and a mission resort. With a one hundred bed capacity, we intended to also create a separate area for physical therapy and sauna. Thankfully, high-quality hot spring mineral water would be available for use at the facility with minimal investment on our part.

For the name of the hospital, we had originally proposed, the Dan Dong Christian Hospital, while the Chinese government had insisted on the Dan Dong Welfare Hospital. Ultimately, the hospital was officially named, the Dan Dong-CMWM Hospital, which, to me, far surpassed our original suggestion, as the name CMWM included the words *Christian*, *welfare*, and *mission*.

Back in the U.S., an intensive "Nehemiah Prayer Campaign" commenced, with the goal of signing up ten thousand prayer members who would make the commitment to pray for the hospital one minute per day, five minutes per week, or at least twenty minutes per month.

As I began speaking out about this new campaign, I was often asked, "What's the difference between this mission and your previous one?" I answered these questions by sharing the following story.

"Not too long ago, a South Korean news program aired a story about a thirteen-year-old orphan boy who had, alone, assumed the responsibility of taking care of his younger brothers after the tragic death of their parents. One Sunday, some elders from the local church initiated an effort to help the boys. The women's mission organization prepared boxes of apples and instant ramen noodles. They arrived on a bus and gave the boxes to the boys, all the while taking many pictures to document their great generosity and good deeds. When the women left, the orphans burst into tears. They wept because they were made to feel like 'monkeys in a zoo' and because they missed their parents.

However, the following day one of the church elders, who had not gone along with the women's group the day before, prepared a home cooked meal and brought it to the boys' home late that afternoon. She washed and fed the orphans. She read them the Bible and stayed with them through the night. Afterward, she visited the boys as frequently as she could. She did this quietly, humbly, of her own volition, without remuneration or recognition. Twenty-five years later, that thirteen-year-old boy grew up to be the principal pastor of one of the largest Korean-American churches in the U.S.

"Is this not a better way of sharing God's love? Our desire is to quietly devote ourselves to this work. We want to be ready to assist the refugees, day or night, to save each and every soul reaching out to us along those treacherous river banks," I explained.

"How long do you intend to do this?" people would ask.

"As long as the Lord wills it and allows us to continue. When He tells us to stop, we will."

I was also determined to do everything within my power to insulate ourselves from the same hurtful outcome that had befallen on us with the Pyong Yang Third Hospital. Painstaking expenditures of time, effort, money, prayers, and tears had amounted to nothingness in the end; I was still expelled from the country after the hospital's completion. I did not want to see the same disastrous fate occur with the Dan Dong Hospital and thought it best to cultivate relationships by aligning ourselves with established and renowned international organizations. Ossifying our base and presence in that volatile region through international support, global partnerships, and recognition would be vital to our survival under the erratic Chinese bureaucracy and enable us to operate the hospital fully according to the Lord's will.

What Are You Doing?

I continued to pray for different assistance avenues for our mission to explore and found myself constantly pondering, How can we help the North Korean refugees beyond just building hospitals?

I was reminded of the Vietnamese boat people during the Vietnam War and recalled how the UNHCR (United Nations High Commissioner for Refugees) had come to their aid. That's it! We need to ask the United Nations for help!

As it so happened, a friend of mine, Pastor Jae Chul Lee, was the head pastor at the Geneva Korean Church in Switzerland at that time; I appealed to him for help. With his assistance, we successfully connected with officers from the UNHCR and Doctors Without Borders, and I received and accepted invitations from both organizations to meet at their respective headquarters. I arranged a trip that would take me first to the UNHCR in Geneva, Switzerland, and then on to Paris, France, for a meeting with representatives from Doctors Without Borders.

When I arrived at the UNHCR, I felt as if I had stepped into a microcosm of the global community. The UN building bustled with activity, populated with individuals of every color and nationality, with English spoken in many different cadences. A coalescence of bright and talented diplomats, lawyers, scientists, and human rights activists agitated for the prioritization and implementation of basic human rights reforms. Each represented their respective governments in the gallant effort to intervene against international oppression and injustice. I envied their youthful energy and admired their broadening understanding of the world through their intellectual voyages and exchanges at the UNHCR.

No less impressive were the protest demonstrations staged outside the UN building. Groups of people, each flowing in the vivid colors of national costumes, took turns in staging impassioned demonstrations that drew on traditional elements of native song and dance to provoke people's awareness of their opposition to global oppression and foreign aggression.

Despite the commotion outside the building, inside, citizens of the world were actively engaged in the orderly exchange of opinions, committed to the challenge of resolving many of the world's most complex social and human rights issues. The war in Kosovo was the key issue of most significance, and the UN's urgent response resulted in medical help and emergency supplies being dispatched immediately to Kosovo. It disturbed me that the same sense of urgency was not being employed in sending aid to the dying North Korean people.

My meeting began with the chief legal counsel for the UNHCR, as well as several other UN lawyers.

"It's believed that the current number of North Korean refugees existing between the borders of North Korea and China is well over three hundred thousand, although that's an approximation, at best. Without assistance, most of these people will die from disease and hunger. North Korean women and children, especially the little girls, are vulnerable victims to severe sexual exploitation and slavery. Many of them are murdered at the hands of their owners. Is there any way to obtain the UNHCR's help in mobilizing efforts to save and assist these people?" I asked.

The chief counsel mulled my question over for a moment and then leaned forward in his seat. He asked me three questions.

"What are you doing for them?"

I went into length describing SAM's medical mission activities and our intent to build the Dan Dong Hospital to assist North Korean refugees escaping over into China via the Yalu and Tumen Rivers.

"What is South Korea doing for them?" he inquired further. My mouth fell open. I had not expected such a question and could give him no good answer.

"I hear that there are many churches in South Korea, but what are those churches doing for the North Korean people?" he pressed on.

My mind screamed with the thoughts that I could not express. Yes, the South Korean churches are currently too busy with their missionary and humanitarian works saving lives in Africa, South America, Southeast Asia, and every other country on the planet to take care of their own North Korean brethren dying right in front of their faces! The entire world was shouting at South Korea to take care of her own, and yet she was ignoring the problem that existed in her very own backyard.

As the meeting wrapped up, I boldly requested for the UNHCR to grant UN refugee status to North Korean refugees subsisting along the Chinese border. This would provide the refugees with the UN's full measure of protection and assistance.

"The Chinese government won't cooperate with us," the chief counsel replied curtly. "They won't allow us to go in and assess the situation along that North Korean and Chinese border. They flatly deny the existence of any refugees from North Korea. Since we can't do anything about it from our end, there has to be more involvement from private NGOs like yours that can."

Although UN recognition for North Korean refugees had not been achieved, the UNHCR did agree to designate SAM, International as one of its nongovernmental organization partners.

The Lilacs

Doctors Without Borders is one of the world's largest medical aid humanitarian organizations. An NGO founded in 1971, it delivers emergency medical aid to people devastated by armed conflicts, famine, epidemics, and natural disasters. In 1995 it was the only private, independent organization granted entrance into North Korea to provide medical help to flood victims. It received the Nobel Peace Prize in 1999.

Following my meeting with the UNHCR officials, I flew to Paris to meet with members of Doctors Without Borders. At the end of a one-hour meeting, they gladly agreed to partner with SAM in helping North Korean refugees along the Chinese-North Korean border. I was so grateful to the Lord, not only for my successful meeting with this organization but also for the opportunity to be in Paris. Being there brought back an onslaught of memories of my student years at Seoul National University Medical School.

On the SNU Medical School campus was a grassy little knoll in front of the Liberal Arts school called Montmartre Hill. Enchantingly beautiful lilac blossoms flourished adjacent to a small, lapping stream called the Seine. I used to go there between my classes to gaze at the splendor of the delicate lilacs and lose myself in their pure beauty. I was always glad to be given a soothing respite from my misery and suffering and a brief rest from my studies.

During my days at SNU Medical School, the routine exhaustion of my unrelenting struggle to overcome oppressive poverty and a hounding sense of endangered survival left me angry at the world. Today as I reflect on those times, I can recall with exact detail the beauty and fragrance of those delicate lilacs and have come to realize that the Lord had been with me during those coldest and darkest of days. His comfort of serene beauty radiated in those quiet moments of welcome relief. Through those lilacs, He gently sustained me through my misery and compelled me forward to this day.

As I made my journey home from Paris, I stopped briefly in South Korea to meet with the Secretary of Unification from the South Korean government. I placed an impassioned plea for help. "There's got to be some way for South Korea to help the North Korean refugees at the national level. If necessary, I'd be willing to informally negotiate with the Chinese government. I plan to establish a medical center on the border of North Korea and China to help save North Korean refugees. Can the South Korean government get actively involved?" I asked.

The secretary leaned back into his seat and assumed a relaxed posture. "The government here can only do so much," he answered casually.

Given the South Korean government's indifference and lack of commitment to mobilize assistance on a national level, I realized that *we* would have to be the ones to do what we could on our own, no matter how small and powerless we were. It was up to us to reach one more life and save one more soul. Yes, let's focus on building the Dan Dong Hospital!

The Publication Ceremony

October 1999. The Dan Dong Hospital construction commenced and almost immediately my phones rang incessantly. Dan Dong, China, and Oakland, California, are at opposite ends of the globe; the middle of the day in Dan Dong is the middle of the night in Oakland. Irrespective of the time of day or night, the calls came without ceasing regarding construction problems, accidents, and money. Sleep became a distant luxury as I answered each call without delay and dealt with the continuous overflow of obstacles. The project had only begun, and I already felt drained.

We were renovating a greatly dilapidated building and were, for all intents and purposes, beginning the construction from scratch. As I was already psychologically depleted from the dramatic events that had transpired with the Pyong Yang Third Hospital in North Korea, I surely would never have been able to bear the monumental scope of this new overwhelming burden without the Lord's fortifying strength,

Costs began spinning frighteningly out of control and we soon found ourselves hurtling at light speed toward insolvency, problems with budgeting and deficit finances far greater than I had ever imagined possible. As a desperate alleviating measure, I put together a book featuring a collection of articles I had written over the years for my newspaper columns on women's health issues and my missionary activities. As the publication date of my book neared, my colleagues and I began brainstorming fundraising events for the Dan Dong Hospital project and decided to blend those conjunctively with the publication ceremonies for my book in a campaign we called "A Night for North Korean Missions." Two events were scheduled: one in Seoul, South Korea, and the other in the U.S.

September 17, 1999. One hundred and fifty people attended the fundraising event held at the Hilton Hotel in Seoul. The venue was packed, as people milled around enjoying delicious food and inspiring company. The main event featured sermons by Pastor Eun Jo Park, who made a tearful plea on behalf of the North Korean refugees, Pastor Jong Tak Ye's challenging message, and my testimonies of my mission trips. Many in the audience were moved to tears and made verbal pledges to support our mission.

By 10:00 p.m. the fundraising event was over, and a few of us had stayed behind to help clean the banquet hall. My cell phone rattled softly in my coat pocket and I answered. It was elder Pak from the SAM-Korea office. She had been in charge of coordinating the evening's event. "Have you had a chance to total the pledges and offerings yet?"

"No, not yet. They're being totaled as we speak," I replied.

Five minutes later she called to ask the same question. I gave her a similar response. Five minutes later she called again to inquire about the pledges. Again, my response was the same. It was not until 11:30 p.m. when the offerings and pledges had finally been completely totaled and recorded, that elder Pak called me again. "Umm, was there anyone who donated $50,000?"

"Yes, one person. How did you know?" I asked.

"HALLELUJAH!" she screamed excitedly over the phone. "Elder Park, God delights in this Dan Dong Hospital project," her voice quivered as she struggled to stay on top of her rising emotions. "I've been praying so hard for a sign from the Lord about this evening and the hospital. As we're in such a difficult position with our current missions budget, I wanted to see if God really wanted us to build this hospital. I had asked the Lord to show me His delight in this project by sending a supporter who would donate $50,000. Specifically that amount!"

How awesome is our God!

In addition, a deacon in attendance that evening pledged $10,000 by way of obtaining a bank loan that she intended to pay back over the course of the following year. The total offerings and pledges coming in from this event amounted to $150,000.

Hallelujah!

A Rare Blessing

Back home in the U.S., SAM-USA planned two publication ceremonies/fundraising events to be held over a two-day period. The response from many was unadulterated skepticism. "It's unrealistic to hold a publication ceremony for two days in the U.S. People have busy lives. A recent book publication ceremony held for a very famous Korean-American author attracted only thirty people. That was actually a decent turnout. You'd better not plan two days. You'll only embarrass yourself!"

I felt discouraged. And yet, I just knew that the Lord took pleasure in this hospital project. I began praying for the attendance of three hundred people for each respective event.

As the days slowly approached, my confidence began waning. My original hope for three hundred people slipped to one hundred fifty. The night before the first event, I hoped for just thirty people. "Dear Lord, I pray that I won't lose face or my dignity entirely. Please send at least thirty people to attend the publication ceremony for my book," I pleaded to the Lord in my early morning prayer.

The Lord spoke to me, "Is your dignity or face that important? Even if just one person attends, are you not able to see my glory in sharing with that one person?"

His words gave me new perspective and filled me with peace.

The first publication ceremony was held at a large church in San Jose. It rained heavily that evening, and as the start time approached, only a few people had sauntered in. My SAM co-workers waited anxiously out by the entrance of the building. We had taken a great leap of faith in preparing enough food to feed two hundred fifty people. As I watched the enormous catered dishes and specialty entrees being carefully arranged on the tables, worry consumed my heart. Who's going to eat all this food?

My wife and I stepped away from the banquet hall and found a deserted room around the corner. We both knelt down to pray. "Dear Jesus, I confess that I may have gone ahead of your will in planning this event. As I humbly kneel before you, I pray that your will be done tonight, no matter how many people show up. Please forgive me, Father. I'm not worthy of your work. I'm a proud sinner, concerned only about saving my reputation. Please transform me into your true and faithful servant." We then sang a hymn together.

I gave my life for thee,
My precious blood I shed,
That thou might'st ransomed be,
And quickened from the dead
I gave, I gave my life for thee,
What hast thou given Me?
I gave, I gave my life for thee,
What hast thou given Me?

Thirty minutes later, my wife and I clasped hands and resolutely walked out of the room. We were ready to joyfully accept whatever

God's will was. As we slowly rounded the corner and made our way back to the banquet hall, a colleague rushed toward us. "Ah! Elder Park, there you are! I've been looking all over for you. It's a miracle. There are over two hundred fifty people in the banquet hall, waiting for the event to start!"

My wife and I looked at each other in stunned amazement.

"JESUS, THANK YOU!" we shouted simultaneously. That night, three people pledged $10,000 each.

The following evening, the second publication ceremony was held in a small community center banquet hall in San Francisco. About thirty to forty people had gathered in the hall by the start time. Table after table displayed elaborate arrays of food and virtually no people. I shrugged and thought to myself, I witnessed the Lord's miracle yesterday. Once is enough.

As on the previous evening, my SAM colleagues went out to the parking lot, hoping to usher in more attendees.

Five minutes passed, ten, then fifteen; more and more guests began trickling in. By the time we were thirty minutes into the worship service, the banquet hall was filled with more than two hundred fifty people. That evening the total number of attendees exceeded four hundred!

The food, originally prepared for two hundred fifty people, did not run out and I was so grateful. It seemed as if Jesus was blessing and multiplying the food as he had with the five barley loaves and two small fish on a mountainside in Israel, thousands of years before.

At midnight the phone woke me. It was Elder Jae Min Lee, from the SAM-USA office. He had been counting and recording the financial pledges made earlier that evening.

"Hallelujah! Elder Park, the Lord is with us. Six people pledged $10,000 each!" he exclaimed excitedly.

"Ah! Thank you, Lord!"

Perhaps the most astonishing factor behind those six pledges was that the people who had made them had done so almost beyond their means. One of the pledges came from a widow who worked days and evenings at a small laundry to support and raise her children. Hearing about such selfless sacrifices, I knelt before the Lord, repenting my weak faith and praying for His special blessings on the precious offerings and the faithful people who had placed them.

The following day the local newspapers reported that the publication ceremonies for my book were the most successful events of their kind in Korean-American history for the San Francisco Bay Area.

Afterward, many wrote to me or called with words of thanks and encouragement: "I'd like to express my sincere thanks to you for giving me a new vision and challenge in my ordinary life"; "I had felt hopeless about the North Korean situation, but you've helped me to see that God's been at work in revealing His glory through all of this"; "Thank you for teaching us how best to commit ourselves to North Korean missions"; "I agree with you on the need to pray for peace and genuine reconciliation between South and North Korea."

During the days following, twenty-seven more people came forward to each donate $10,000 or more for our hospital project. I was so humbled and thankful for the trust and faith people had placed in our mission. I pledged to push myself more fervently and press on with more resolve in overseeing the Dan Dong Hospital construction and our other mission activities, lest I betray the trust of these people in any way.

I Did Not Want to Die

As we continued to seek support from international organizations, Doctors Without Borders joined us on one of our 750-mile vision trips. Four doctors from the organization (originally from France, the Netherlands, Australia, and Denmark) joined us to form a twenty-five-person team for the mission.

Our arrival on a bus to Jang Baek, China, stirred great excitement among the villagers. The presence of Western doctors provoked curiosity and attracted many people in this isolated farming community to our small field clinics. Once we began treating patients, many more flocked to seek our help.

The European doctors were very humble and open minded. They did not carry much luggage with them, just one backpack each. Yet, they seemed prepared to go anywhere and do anything in order to accomplish their work. Jang Baek was a rural village with no modern facilities or plumbing. Foul, filthy holes in the dirt served as toilets and reeked badly. However, none of the doctors complained about the difficult living conditions. Although they did not participate in any of our worship services, the doctors generously obliged each patient with time, great kindness, and care.

For ten days we treated patients during the day and in the evenings shared with the European doctors our knowledge about the North Korean refugees. I thought it important for them to clearly understand the urgent, perilous plight of the refugees. Through some of our missionaries working in that region, I made arrangements for them to meet a nineteen-year-old North Korean refugee who had recently crossed the border in desperate search of food and medicine for his family.

"LONG LIVE OUR GREAT LEADER PRESIDENT KIM IL SUNG!" The young North Korean refugee was shouting boldly, a possessed expression was etched on his face, and he startled everyone in the room.

The physicians from Doctors Without Borders had taken time out of conducting clinics to meet with the refugee. I was shocked and began suspecting that the young refugee might actually be a North Korean agent stealthily masquerading as a refugee. It was outrageous and incomprehensible for any reasonably thinking person to praise a regime that had allowed millions of its own people to starve to death under its rule.

The European doctors began asking the young man many questions. "We've heard of many traumatic experiences of the North Korean refugees. Aren't they true?"

"Those aren't true at all. Thanks to our Great General's leadership, the North Korean people live in the greatest paradise on earth!" the young man stated defiantly.

"That's contrary to what we've heard. Aren't many North Koreans trying to leave the country in order to escape starvation and persecution?"

"Absolutely not. That is false. There is plenty to eat."

I felt my temper rising; I wanted to slap the young man in the face.

Perplexed, the doctors turned to me and asked, "Hey, Dr. Park, what's going on here? This is much different from what we've heard and what you've been telling us."

I was at an utter loss for words and could think of no quick response.

The doctors quietly returned to their quarters and I stayed behind in the room, bewildered by what had just transpired. We could not have had a better occasion to illuminate with a firsthand account the horrors and atrocities of what was actually occurring inside of North Korea. Additionally, the young man had no inkling as to how crucial it was for us as an organization to obtain the partnership of Doctors Without Borders in setting up clinics along the Tumen and Yalu Rivers. My heart ached at the seemingly lost opportunity.

As I turned back in disbelief, the young refugee ran toward me and burst into tears.

"Dear Doctor, I'm so sorry. I just . . . ." He wept harder. "I just yelled the government slogans to save my life. My life has always been at risk, and when you had originally asked me to meet with the doctors, I thought that I would be speaking to one or two people.

But when I saw so many people here, including the Westerners, I became frightened for my life. I did not want to die, even though I deserve to die. I know I don't have the right to ask this of you, but I'm here to get medicine for my mother and younger brother who are both dying of tuberculosis. Please save my mother and brother."

I was so angry and disgusted, but I could not hate him. How desperate this young man must be, I thought as I drew him close and wrapped my arms around him. He continued to sob remorsefully.

The following day, I shared the young man's story with everyone during our early morning quiet time. All who were present broke down into tears, including the physicians from Doctors Without Borders.

Later that same day the doctors informed me, "We've called our headquarters in Paris to recommend that our organization work here with you."

If the Lord pleases, nothing is impossible!

Manmandi, "To Behave as They Saw Fit"

Given the stark contrasts in language, culture, and ethics, building a hospital in China was an extremely convoluted and frustrating process. Dealing with the Chinese proved to be as challenging and difficult as dealing with the North Koreans, in every way.

I had originally thought that the definition of the Chinese word *manmandi* meant to do things slowly. I soon learned that for the Chinese, *manmandi* meant not only doing things slowly but also doing things their way, however they wished, no matter how lengthy the process.

Chinese construction laborers did not have any sense of timeliness, deadlines, or boundaries. They seemed to disdain honest work ethics, a habit possibly acquired under communist rule. Whatever we contracted with them inevitably entailed an exorbitant wait before any work actually commenced or was completed. Whatever the outcome, good, bad, mediocre, they were always in the right and we had no say. We were continually reminded that we were in *their* country; therefore, we needed to assimilate ourselves to their rules and adopt their ways. Like it or not; take it or leave it.

They behaved as they saw fit.

We were subjected to much abuse and cheated many times over by the Chinese workers during the building of the Dan Dong Hospital. Many receipts were concocted and fraud became rampant.

Winter construction was prone to strange and suspicious mishaps. Newly installed pipes froze and burst and had to be reinstalled. The exterior paint job did not dry in the frigid winter temperatures and had to be repainted—seven times!

At the start of the construction, we had received a sizeable donation of hundreds of drums of paint from an American paint company, enough paint to last us for many years beyond the construction completion. However, after the application of just one coat of paint (the use of twelve drums) the Chinese construction manager reported that the entire paint supply had simply run out. Supposedly, there were no more drums of paint left. An impossibility! We searched frantically for the missing paint drums, to no avail. They had mysteriously vanished and we had no choice but to purchase more, with each repainting of the building.

According to the xenophobic Chinese officials, they had extended our organization a magnanimous favor in allowing foreigners to build a hospital on Chinese soil. They demanded extra money every step along the way. Nothing was ever accomplished without first "greasing their palms." Sometimes officials would refuse to meet with us unless they had first received their payment to do so.

At the start, our entire projected budget for the hospital construction was $800,000. But with the unexpected costs, the final construction bill came to over $1,200,000.

I was unsure as to whether the Chinese practice of faked receipts, fraudulent claims, and scamming work ethics were any better than what went on in North Korea, where whole shipping containers of food aid could suddenly disappear or be misappropriated without any accountability.

To me, they were the same.

Scandal at the Dan Dong Hospital

It was 2:00 a.m. when the phone woke me. "Hello?" I mumbled, half asleep.

"Elder Park! Have you heard? There's great trouble at Dan Dong!" It was Deacon Chae from one of our largest supporting churches in South Korea. The deacon's voice was sharp and terse.

"What do you mean *trouble*? What kind of trouble?" I was wide awake.

"Rumor has it that the hospital construction site has become a place for drinking parties. It's scandalous, and people here are in an absolute uproar about it."

"What do you mean?" I asked in disbelief and swung my legs quickly over the side of the bed.

"It's the young evangelist who came from South Korea to supervise the construction workers. We've heard that he's been drinking with the Chinese workers. A few days ago a well-known South Korean gospel group toured the hospital construction site and they witnessed the alcohol and the drunkeness. And now the news is spreading like wildfire to the other SAM-supporting churches."

"Oh my goodness!" I gasped. I could not believe what I had just heard. The young evangelist had been sent by a South Korean church to help oversee the construction process. It was inconceivable that he would have made the decision to serve without a firm dedication and deep commitment to the Lord's mission. Something must have been misunderstood.

I placed an immediate phone call to Dan Dong to speak to the young man.

"Elder Park, I'm awfully sorry . . . I think I was too ignorant of Chinese traditions. The Chinese workers wouldn't work. They just sat around and complained constantly about being hungry and thirsty. They kept telling me they needed liquor. I thought that if I bought them some, maybe they would be motivated to work. But I was naïve about Chinese drinking culture. The Chinese find it disrespectful to not share drinks. What could I do? Even though I kept insisting that I didn't want to drink, they wouldn't accept my answer. I was coerced into drinking a few cups, and, well, I have no tolerance for alcohol, and my face turned bright red. That's when . . . the gospel group happened to appear. I'm deeply sorry. I'm really not the kind of person who drinks."

I did not know what to say in response. I could understand how this well-meaning but very naïve and foolish evangelist fell into this situation, but I also knew that there would be irreparable consequences because of this silly incident. As it turned out, the rumor persisted and refused to go away; and, as a result, many financial supporters, including the Christian gospel group that had surveyed the hospital construction, discontinued their financial support for our mission.

Celebrating the opening of the Dan Dong Hospital

Welcoming our guests at the opening ceremony

8

Dan Dong is the New Canaan

It was early April. Two hundred people from the U.S., South Korea, and Europe were gathering in Dan Dong, in preparation to attend the opening ceremony of the Dan Dong Hospital, which was to be held on April 13, 2000. I had arrived in Shen Yang, China, earlier in the week to spend some time in worship services with some North Korean refugees we had been quietly assisting.

I felt as if we were assembling together, poising ourselves to finally enter the Promised Land of Canaan.

In a sense, Dan Dong could be called the modern-day Canaan.

I likened the struggles endured in our mission—before the existence of the Dan Dong Hospital—to that of the aimless wandering of the Israelites in the rugged wilderness before their entrance into God's Promised Land. Journeying from Egypt to Canaan, the Israelites roamed for forty years, a distance that could easily have been traversed in eleven days. The Lord diverted the Israelites and prevented their direct entrance into the Promised Land, because He knew they were not ready.

Twelve years had passed since I had embarked on my very first trip into North Korea. Since that time the Lord had continually prepared me, molded me, trained me, and transformed me. He saw me through many jubilant triumphs and spiraling downfalls. I had traveled into North Korea on more than twenty trips, too often caught between the unrealistic expectations of overzealous sponsors, discontented colleagues, and the preposterous demands of the perfidious North Korean officials. I found myself constantly in the heat of hostile exchanges and contentious negotiations. After each trip into North Korea, I repeatedly promised myself, "This is the last time! This is it! I quit!"

I engaged in many risks to pursue this work. I trusted certain individuals only to be betrayed by them. I relinquished my profession and left behind thirty years of my respectable, comfortable life. Additionally, my children were hurled into a predicament they could never have foreseen or asked for: parents who sometimes missed pivotal, life-defining moments in their lives. I uprooted our family for a missionary life on the volatile outskirts of a foreign land, while approaching an age when most people hunkered down for a relaxing retirement.

None of these had been easy for me or my family to do.

Too often, I wished to run away from this work. And yet, the Lord always kept me steady in the face of frighteningly tempestuous storms. He gently cheered me on to faithfully follow Him and mollified my angst with His soothing comfort. I complained. I rebelled. I cried. And still the Lord remained patient with me, covering my sinfulness, shortcomings, and glaring faults with His veil of lovingkindness.

I do not enjoy a comfortable doctor's life of prosperity or pleasure pursuing this mission. But I am infused with an overwhelming joy and peace that surpasses all understanding and true richness that come from sharing Christ with others. The privilege and honor of serving our Lord in this capacity, bringing glory to His name, outranks the luxurious comforts and tangible amenities of this very temporary life.

The Lord showed me the importance of establishing a mission center at the border regions, a place where suffering North Korean people would be in reachable distance of the sanctuary of our hospital and live. It is He who planted the vision of training Korean Russians, Korean Chinese, and North Korean refugees living in those border regions to rise up and one day become His missionaries for the world, emissaries for His kingdom.

Twelve years after I began my missionary work in North Korea, the Lord finally led us to the Dan Dong Hospital. This is why Dan Dong was like Canaan to me.

The Dan Dong Hospital was established to be a place where those weary of the wilderness of Russia, China, and North Korea could come and rest their bodies and refresh their souls. May Dan Dong become the Canaan of the twenty-first century from where we are able to proselytize and send out future ambassadors of the Lord to the farthest corners of the world. May our efforts at the Dan Dong Hospital have far-reaching implications that affect not only the here and now but for an eternity. May we become beacons of His light for people all around the world.

"Be strong and courageous. Be not terrified; be not discouraged"
(Joshua 1:6).

The Official Opening of the Dan Dong Hospital

April 13, 2000. With the commencement of the opening ceremony, the Dan Dong Hospital officially opened its doors. Among the two hundred honored guests and supporters in attendance were thirty pastors from South Korea and the U.S., as well as five European doctors from Doctors Without Borders. I greeted our guests at the ceremony with great enthusiasm. "Welcome to our international hospital, where people of all nationalities—Chinese, Koreans, Americans, and Europeans—will work together to save lives. May the Dan Dong Hospital become a place of healing and rest for each and every person who comes to visit."

As the opening ceremony festivities proceeded, concurrently, we had arranged for a cavalcade of trucks loaded with food and medicine to cross the Yalu River Bridge into North Korea. With our new Dan Dong Hospital now firmly established, we were in a position to help people on both sides of the Yalu River. No longer would we be limited by the smothering constraints of working only inside of North Korea. If our access to the suffering people inside the country was limited, we would wait for those North Korean refugees crossing the Yalu River to reach the safety of our hospital and directly receive our assistance.

Immediately following the ceremony, the pastors in attendance gathered together to conduct a baptismal service for Joo Il Sang, the baby boy born to the North Korean woman we had rescued from slavery. We prayed for the woman and child and asked the Lord to envelop them in His loving grace. As I held the tiny infant in my arms, he looked up at me with large wondering eyes and cooed adorably. He was so lovely. I felt as if I was holding my own grandson. In a sense, he was indeed my grandson, my spiritual grandson. He was the first North Korean refugee child to be baptized at the Dan Dong Hospital. I trusted the Lord's goodness would follow him all the days of his life. It was surely the Lord's grace that led us to meet him in the first place.

Three days later, my colleagues and I boarded a boat that sailed along the length of the Yalu River. The engine chugged noisily as the vessel puttered through choppy waters, hugging the grim, bleak shoreline of Sin Eu Ju, North Korea. The residents stared blankly at us as we passed by.

"HELLO!" we shouted.

No one responded except a lone woman who had been washing her clothes in the river. She raised her child's arm and waved it at us. We shouted to her in unison.

"WE LOVE YOU!"

We held an emotional worship service in the boat as our hands stretched out toward the barren North Korean shores. The sound of our pleading prayers rose off the misty water in mournful wails.

That night, we expanded our worship with an evening service at the Dan Dong Hospital chapel. Two hundred fifty of us gathered together to pray, worship, and seek the Lord. We wept and cried out for His mercy, "Please save these people. Please save their souls."

The next morning, the physicians from Doctors Without Borders politely informed me of their intent to disassociate themselves from SAM. "We were quite taken aback last night. Our organization isn't associated or affiliated with any religion whatsoever. We actually can't be working with any religious organizations. It seems clear to us that we won't be able to work with SAM anymore."

I had no choice but to accept their decision. They left immediately.

During the first week of the hospital's official opening, the Chinese police began the first of what would eventually become countless intrusive searches of the facility for the same reason: suspicion of religious activity.

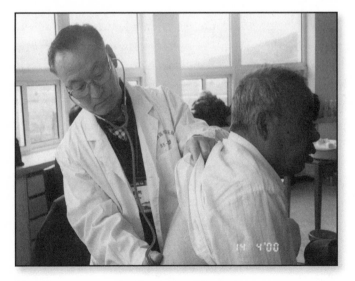

Treating patients at the Dan Dong Hospital

Siege at the Dan Dong Hospital

The medical services offered to the patients at the Dan Dong Hospital were entirely free of charge. Our objective was not monetary gain, but to save lives. Each day, throngs of people flocked to our hospital for help. In the early mornings it was not uncommon for our staff to find a dense crowd of people huddled outside by the entrance, before the hospital even opened its doors for the day, waiting to be helped.

One afternoon as the hospital was abuzz with activity—doctors treating patients, a waiting room crowded with people—the Chinese police invaded the hospital and conducted a sweeping search.

"Dr. Park, the Chinese police raided our hospital today!"

The alarming news came just as I was about to preach a two-day revival at the San Diego Methodist Church. "They raided our hospital and repeatedly questioned us as to why we would run a free facility. They wanted to know why we wouldn't want to make money. They insinuated that if we're not here to make money, then we must be here for missionary purposes. They threatened to arrest us and demanded that each of our doctors submit a list of names of people who've been proselytizing. Because they didn't find any incriminating evidence during the raid, they're now summoning you. They may arrest us if you don't come. What should we do?"

The news momentarily froze my heart and lungs and I could not think, breathe, or feel.

It was because of the powerfully intimidating force exercised by the Chinese military that the bifurcated system of communist politics still dominated amid more liberal and global economic policies. China's police force was formidable and frightening. I had once witnessed a public execution of two criminals in the middle of downtown Shen Yang in broad daylight. The memory of it still remained terribly traumatic in my mind.

That same police force had invaded and plundered our hospital. And now they were coming after me.

I no longer had the presence of mind to give a sermon and wanted to cancel the entire revival meeting. On my way to the church, I called many places, looking for assistance, including the South Korean Embassy.

As the time for my testimony quickly approached, my mind was immersed in chaotic tumult. And panic. How do I protect the people working at the hospital? How do I protect myself? I was a pitiful sight, as my confidence dissolved away with every petrifying minute. "Dear Jesus, I'm terrified for the many people at the hospital; I'm terrified for myself. Given my current state of mind, how can I be of any help to those who are gathered here tonight to listen to my testimony?"

The Lord's gentle voice of comfort spoke to me: "You've had over sixty years of life in God's grace. Should you still be so afraid to die?"

The thought of our Lord scourged and wounded, painfully carrying His cross to the dark hills of Golgotha to die, came to mind. "Since I've overcome the world, be brave and courageous. There is nothing to fear," the Lord assured me.

I went to the pulpit feeling nauseous and in tears. "I'm the lowest of men, a weak sinner, and small in faith. I don't deserve to stand before you," I confessed to the congregation.

The congregants responded with great favor to my testimony. The Lord's anointing grace cradled the service as we lifted our prayers and praises as one. Tears of repentance flowed.

Immediately after the revival, Elder Jae Min Lee and I flew to Shen Yang, China. We were on our way to the Dan Dong Hospital by car when my cell phone rang.

"Dr. Park, you mustn't come to the hospital. If you do, you'll be arrested right away!" warned one of our missionaries.

We spent the night in a little hotel in downtown Dan Dong, near the hospital. My mind was fraught with worry for my colleagues still being detained. Unsurprisingly, Elder Lee and I lay awake for hours, sleep being no match for fear. At 3:00 a.m. we rose out of bed and prayed together until the sun's first light illuminated our room. Our anxiety relented as the Lord brought peace to our panic-filled hearts.

Later that morning, we made half a dozen phone calls to influential Chinese citizens who were active supporters of the Dan Dong Hospital, pleading for advice and assistance. It was pointless to hide away in a hotel, we were told. All hotels in China were required to report the passport numbers of their guests to government authorities within one hour of check-in. Most likely, the police already knew where we were.

Later that afternoon, I braced myself for the worst and prayerfully made my way to the hospital. To my great shock and relief, the Chinese police greatly toned down their terrorizing posture. They did not arrest me or any of our missionaries. Mercifully, nothing terrible happened. Still, the Chinese police threatened to arrest us and shut down our hospital if we did not stop providing free medical care. They demanded that we start charging patients for our services. We had no choice but to comply.

It was some time later that I learned that the police raid had come as a result of one of my most trusted colleagues at the hospital, tipping off the police about our Christian activities. To my great disbelief, this individual had betrayed us in the hopes of taking over the hospital for himself.

He had betrayed us for power and prestige.

Through such harrowing trials, my faith continues to be refined and strengthened. The Lord has shown me in every situation, in every corner of the globe, He is with me, walking beside me, and carrying me through when I have no strength to carry myself. Today I have confidence in living and working in China. I no longer fear the Chinese police, nor do I fear losing the Dan Dong Hospital or of being expelled from the country. Nobody knows what tomorrow holds. Surrendering all things to Him has brought the dawning realization that the privilege of intimately knowing, obediently serving, and loving the Lord Jesus Christ is more precious than life itself.

The Lord Leads Us to Jian

September 2000. The Dan Dong Hospital stopped providing free medical services, and soon after, the hospital became eerily quiet, empty, and devoid of patients. Many of the poor and destitute villagers who wished to receive our medical care could no longer afford to come to our hospital as they possessed no money to pay the minimal fees we were now forced to charge patients. Additionally, the SARS epidemic raged globally, igniting a firestorm of frenzied panic and blatant misinformation. Hospitals and medical facilities became macabre places, in the minds of many who adhered to the erroneous notion that infection by the SARS virus could occur by simply being present in the same medical facility in which other SARS patients were being treated.

If the patients could not or would not come to us, we would go to them.

Our plan was to send our doctors to the most remote and rural regions along the Yalu and Tumen Rivers to visit patients. Additionally, we desired to set up a series of small clinics along the river banks, similar to the one we had set up in Ussrisk, Russia.

A group of doctors and I embarked on our fifth medical outreach to those removed areas. We would be providing medical services and scouting potential locations for our small medical outposts. Our first destination was Jang Baek, China. Jang Baek was an isolated and bucolic village far removed and difficult to reach. People living in this rural community had very primitive standards of living and no access to medical care, which made it clear to us that a clinic should definitely be set up there.

Another possible clinic site that came to my mind was Samhap. I recalled a large bridge in Samhap, which spanned the border between

North Korea and China. I had encountered this bridge years ago while embarking on a medical mission to Najin Sunbong. I thought that setting up a clinic at Samhap would also be necessary.

A few days after conducting clinics in Jang Baek, I sent two of my colleagues to Samhap to survey the area while the rest of our team headed back to the Dan Dong Hospital. They called a few hours later to make a report. "Dr. Park, we've just found a place called Jian. We've discovered that, historically, it's a very important city. Would you consider establishing a clinic here?"

Though they were recommending an unexpected place called Jian, I misunderstood and thought they had said Samhap. Due to the loud rumbling noises coming from our bus engine and the crescendo of conversations surrounding me, I had misheard them.

"Yes, let's set up a clinic there," I said, giving my immediate approval.

"Then, instead of going directly back to Dan Dong, could you stop by here first?"

That was odd, I thought. Their suggestion wasn't consistent with my knowledge of the geography.

"Isn't Samhap located in the far north? That's a journey of at least several days. How would I be able to stop by there on my way to Dan Dong? And now that I think about it, how did you get there so quickly?" I asked puzzled.

"Pardon me? No, it's surely on your way back."

I asked them again. Something was surely wrong. "Didn't you say Samhap?"

"I'm sorry. Did you say Samhap? No, I said Jian. You agreed to the idea of setting up a clinic in Jian."

I realized that I had been confused. "No . . . I meant Samhap."

"No, you spoke of Jian."

"All right. If that's the case, we'll just go and survey Jian," I relented.

We arrived at Jian a few hours later. As we surveyed the richly dense landscape, my colleagues and I were overwhelmed by the essence of our Korean ancestry and heritage that permeated the air. The area was fertile with the inexplicable energy and mystical presence of the Koguryo Dynasty that had ruled over seven hundred years ago. Mesmerized, we stood before mammoth sized stone structures that had remained preserved for centuries as enduring evidence of ancient Korean kingdoms and ruling clans

"Yes! Let's open a clinic here!" we agreed unanimously.

The view was breathtaking. The mid-day sun glistened brilliantly on the Yalu River and from our vantage point, standing along a plateau high above the water, we were looking straight down on a North Korean city.

"O, Lord," I gasped, awed by the manner in which He had led us there. A seeming mistake, hearing the word *Jian* for *Samhap*, had put us there.

Astonishing!

Trumpeters of the Gospel

Through our hospitals and clinics, we provide medical services and assistance. However, this represents but a small means of our true mission: sharing the gift of salvation through the gospel of our Lord Jesus Christ.

We desire to physically heal and nurture the sick, to lavish with love, those who have never known love before. However, beyond the physical healing we proffer, the significance of the gospel is where true healing lies. It is of paramount import to raise up, train, and disciple those individuals who have the ability to someday return to North Korea as "trumpeters of the gospel."

Bible study and discipleship training programs have been implemented at our riverside clinics. The Lord's anointed blessings over these programs have produced astonishing results—formidable orchestras of trumpeters now herald His good news! One afternoon, during a particular worship service at one of the clinics, one hundred people came forward to be baptized and publicly declare their new-found faith in Christ!

It was an early October day and the weather was unseasonably cold. A medical colleague and I sat outside one of our clinics along the Tumen River. We had tended to patients all morning and were now enjoying a brief respite in our schedule. We attempted to warm ourselves in a weak patch of sunlight and our fingers wrapped around steaming cups of coffee. My colleague took a long sip from his cup and reclined into his chair. "I've got the most amazing testimony to share with you," he said as he stretched his legs out before him. A lazy grin came over his face, and I knew that I was in for quite a story.

"Last year a young North Korean woman escaped and came to us for help. She was in desperate shape . . . starving, sick. Of course, we found her a safe place to stay and got her all the basics, food, clothes, Bible. She was so frightened of being caught that she remained holed up in her room all day long. She wouldn't leave. She did nothing but read the Bible we'd given her. Well, later she signed up for our Bible study and discipleship program and came to accept Christ and got saved. She then became desperate to go back to North Korea. She had a pressing burden to share the gospel with her family and friends back home and was more than willing to risk her life to do it. Gosh, we spent so much time in prayer with her before she left, and then before we knew it, she was gone. She left for North Korea, clutching that Bible we'd given her, close to her chest as she crossed the Tumen River.

"Afterward, we never stopped praying for her. We hoped that she was alive and safe, but, of course, there was no way of knowing. Approximately a year later, she made her way back to see us. What a miracle that was! There were hugs and tears all around. When we asked how she'd been all that time, she couldn't stop crying as she told us what happened: 'On my way back into North Korea,

I was caught by the North Korean border guards. They found the Bible that I was carrying and tortured me to try to get me to confess how I'd gotten the book. They wanted names, and I wasn't about to reveal any. To try to break my will, they tore out my fingernails and I must've blacked out from the pain. Strangely, by the time I'd regained consciousness, I couldn't feel anything. The border guards continued to torture me, and as the face of the young soldier abusing me loomed large before me, all of a sudden, his face was replaced by the very face of our Lord Jesus Christ. Our Lord was weeping, with large tears streaming down His face.

"I was sent to a grueling concentration camp and spent three months there. After I got released, I started an underground church that I call Stephen's Church in my hometown. We have a total of seven members. It's way too dangerous for us to meet all at once. We usually try to meet in groups of two every day. We're praying for the day when every North Korean man, woman, and child is able to hear the gospel and know our Lord Jesus Christ."

My colleague's eyes moistened as he continued, "I felt so ashamed of myself as she told her story. . . . She kept her faith even as they tore out her fingernails." He shook his head as his voice became choked with emotion. "With her faith still in a gestational place, she exhibited more godly strength and endurance than people who've been Christians their whole lives. I've never had to encounter such persecution, and after her story, I felt stupid for all the petty things I'd been complaining about. . . . I know that I've complained too much about our living conditions here in China. . . . This refugee comes back to see us pretty often to get more Bible knowledge and risks her life every single time she does. It's amazing."

Such precious transformations are the singular reason why my colleagues and I are here to serve the Lord in this capacity. This woman's testimony is powerful evidence of God's divine plan to unleash His saving power and healing grace throughout all of North Korea.

Stealth surveillance and intense scrutiny characterizes the oppressive environment of life along the North Korean and Chinese border regions. The Chinese police and North Korean secret agents furtively mill around conducting sinister campaigns of cruelty and domination. With danger lurking around every corner, North Korean refugees very often have no alternative but to return to North Korea, paradoxically, to survive.

Before sending the refugees back to North Korea, we provide them with the equivalent of $300. If they should be caught by the border guards during re-entry, $100 is to be used to try to negotiate their release. The remaining $200 is enough to feed and clothe a North Korean family of six abundantly for one year. With each refugee returning back home, we impress on them the following counsel, "Take good care of yourselves. Stay alive and healthy. You have a very important responsibility. You are now a trumpeter of the gospel."

The vision the Lord has planted in our hearts for North Korea has given birth to our clinic missions and has gained unstoppable momentum. We now have three clinical outposts: Ussrisk, Russia; Jang Baek, China; and Jian, China. From these clinic missions, we support over one hundred fifty underground churches along the region. It is our prayer and hope to eventually send medical missionaries to each and every community along the Tumen and Yalu Rivers and, someday, to the farthest corners of the globe.

The Cross

November 2000. We designated a small room in the Dan Dong Hospital to serve as a chapel for prayer and worship services. Doing so was an enormous risk, and we went to great lengths to keep the existence of the chapel hidden from outsiders. If knowledge of our prayer services ever reached the Chinese police, a fiery unleashing of explosive problems would have resulted. This was something that I would never have dared to attempt at the Pyong Yang Third Hospital in North Korea.

On the front wall of the chapel, we erected a small wooden cross. The cross was remarkable. It had been made out of random branches collected from a chestnut tree on a small hill just behind the hospital. The branches had been bound together with twine and shaped to form a rudimentary cross that was unadorned and simple, plain and beautiful. From this imperfect cross radiated the very perfect presence of our Lord.

The arms curved slightly, bending inward at the ends, which often reminded me of our Lord Jesus' outstretched arms, inviting us to Him for comfort, solace, strength. The Lord's petitioning whispers on our behalf seemed to emanate, *"Holy Father, protect them by the power of your name—the name you gave me—so that they may be one as we are one" (John 17:11).*

The tip of the cross leaned forward, slightly askew, as if the Lord's head was bowed in supplication. The pronounced knuckle at the knee of the cross stirred images of Jesus kneeling in prayer.

"In the same way, the Spirit helps us in our weakness. We do not know what we ought to pray for, but the Spirit himself intercedes for us with groans that words cannot express" (Romans 8:26).

The very first day the cross was erected, my colleagues and I were in the middle of a peaceful morning worship when a phone call shattered our serenity and spawned feelings of immense fear. It was the Chinese police. "We're watching you! Take the cross down now!" they ordered.

Alarmed, we took down the cross immediately. As our shock began to dissipate, questions began to form. We had just put up the cross. How did they find out? For subsequent services, we discreetly hung the cross only during worship services and immediately hid it afterward.

After a month or so of doing this, we heard nothing further from the Chinese police. Cautiously, we began to keep the cross up for several weeks at a time. Again, we heard nothing from the police.

Since that time we have had no further communications about the cross from the Chinese police, and it has remained erected on the front wall without interruption. My colleagues and I have unanimously concluded: This cross must stay up despite any difficulties we may encounter because of it. However, for quite some time, we kept the chapel door locked during our worship services.

Not long ago I received the following memo:

"I'm one of the employees of the Dan Dong Hospital. It was, I, who reported the existence of the chapel and the cross to the police."

I was shocked and disheartened by the fact that there was someone inside our hospital spying for the authorities. I also felt greatly saddened by the thought that we might have to suspect all the Chinese employees working for us.

The memo ended, however, with an astonishing confession: "I was ordered by the Chinese Party to function as their informant while here in the hospital. I'm sorry, but I had no choice in the matter. But I'd like to confess to you that I've been greatly affected by the good works you and your fellow doctors do here and have decided to become a believer of Jesus Christ."

I did not know who this person was and did not have to know. The grace of our Lord was affecting change in those who had originally intended us harm. The Lord was working out all things for our own good, and His majesty was being gloriously displayed in the process. And because of this, we were emboldened to remain courageous and faithful, even under the constant scrutiny of probing and suspicious eyes.

Worship at the Dan Dong Hospital chapel

The Cross Necklace

November 2000. My wife and I had just finished breakfast when she placed an object in my hands. It was a gold cross necklace. "I'd like for you to wear it," she said.

I was about to embark on a whirlwind trip to China and South Korea for the next nine days, and she was worried about the frenzied pace of my schedule. I would be flying to Dan Dong to supervise the completion of a second dental clinic at the hospital and meeting with sixty pastors who were coming to see our work there. I would then be flying back to South Korea to preach at five different churches.

"My mother gave me this necklace, and I want you to wear it. I've been praying over it. As you wear it, may the Lord greatly bless all that you do and keep you healthy."

"You know how much I hate wearing jewelry," I reminded her. I never wore necklaces. In fact, I greatly disliked being encumbered with jewelry of any kind, but she was determined to see me wear this one. I relented and allowed her to clasp the thin necklace around my neck. I'll just wear it for now and take it off once I get on the plane, I told myself.

Having just returned from a lengthy testimonial trip to Seoul three weeks before, I now found myself returning to Dan Dong once again. As I sat on the plane, waiting for my flight to take off, I began to feel ill. Surprisingly, remembering that I still wore the cross necklace reminded me of the Lord's constant nearness and brought about an immediate sense of calm.

Heavy winter had settled early on the Korean Peninsula. All flights from Incheon Airport to Shen Yang, China, had been cancelled due to a massive snow storm. Working against an extremely tight schedule with no time to spare, I decided to travel to Dan Dong by way of ship.

The vessel was filled with merchant peddlers who frequently traveled the Yellow Sea from South Korea to China. "The boat will rock badly in the rough seas tonight. You'd better fill your stomach with food now, or you're sure to get nauseous," they warned.

Already feeling queasy, the thought of food was extremely unappealing. Accepting the unpleasant notion that seasickness would most likely plague me at some point during the trip, I took medicine in an attempt to offset any possible symptoms and went to my quarters to lie down.

Two hours after our departure from Incheon, we encountered a turbulent and howling storm. Roaring waves rose to terrifying heights, as the ship crashed and heaved violently with each gigantic swell. I tried desperately to shut out the storm by sleeping, but instead, tossed and turned in the dark, barely able to shut my eyes for fear. The heater in my room began blowing out cold air, and as I rose from my bed to switch it off, a sudden urge to vomit overcame me. I lay back down and buried my head miserably into my pillow.

Is this how Jonah felt as he sat imprisoned in a dark, slimy, smelly whale? I wondered. Suddenly, I remembered my cross necklace with its tiny figure of our Lord Jesus emblazoned on it. Jesus had admonished His twelve disciples for being so frightened and faithless during a violent storm.

"Ah, Lord, you're with me. Jesus, thank you," I whispered as I fingered the precious necklace. As I did so, God's warmth enveloped me, embraced me, protected me. Mercifully, He draped me with His veil of soothing peace.

Ah! My wife knew that I would need this cross. "Thank you, honey, thank you dear mother-in-law," I whispered. Amid the raging and turbulent seas, I managed to fall soundly asleep, enwrapped in the Lord's beautiful presence.

The next morning my arrival at the Dan Dong Hospital caught everyone by surprise. "We tried to get to Shen Yang Airport yesterday to pick you up, but the roads were too icy. In fact, we almost got stranded on a steep hill," a colleague said.

"Jesus allowed me to walk across the water," I said with a wink and a smile. Everyone laughed.

I met with sixty pastors and elders from Seoul. They had originally come to just survey and tour the Dan Dong Hospital, but as I shared my testimonies, going into depth about our mission, they collectively made a $60,000 donation. We used those funds to buy an ambulance.

After wrapping up my Dan Dong schedule, I boarded a plane back to South Korea. I preached at the Seoul Central Methodist Church during the Sunday morning service. It was the first time a layman had preached the Sunday service in its one hundred-year history. They had once donated two dental clinics for the Pyong Yang Third Hospital in North Korea. And now this church supported our SAM mission by sending a missionary couple to serve at the Dan Dong Hospital. After the service, the church pledged to continue with their generous support for our mission.

Later that afternoon, I spoke at the Duksu Church, which pledged to provide an additional dental clinic for the Dan Dong Hospital. The following Monday, I traveled to Daegu to lead a pastoral seminar. On Tuesday, I led two prayer meetings in the early morning hours in two separate cities. Afterward, a mad dash to the airport was made to catch a plane home.

I had begun this trip fatigued and weary; I returned home refreshed and energized. The very next morning I resumed my full schedule of seeing and treating patients at the Northern California VA Hospital. The cross necklace had comforted me through stormy seas and a punishing, jam-packed schedule. It had served as an encouraging reminder that Jesus would keep me from drowning in my own busyness, fatigue, and fear.

Thanks to the loving prayers and infinite wisdom of my dear wife!

9

I Did Not Come Here Just To Get Medicine

Twenty of us embarked on another medical mission trip to Jang Baek. We spent our days conducting clinics and treating patients, which often numbered well over two hundred a day. One evening as I washed my hands, feeling exhausted and hungry, a man approached me apologetically. Perhaps I looked least likely to complain about helping him at that hour. Perhaps I looked too tired to object.

As he sat down, I asked flatly, "Where are you hurting?"

"I have a headache, back pain, heart problems, and I'm constantly feeling run down."

Oh brother! This guy didn't need just a doctor, he needed an entire hospital. "Okay, I understand," I said without the slightest trace of empathy.

I gave him the speediest of check-ups and quickly scribbled out a prescription for him. "You can pick up your medicines at the pharmacy on your way out." Now finally, I could get something to eat!

He looked down meekly at the prescription I had just placed in his hand. "In order to meet you today, I left my home at four in the morning, walked two hours to catch a five-hour train ride, and then took a bus for three hours to arrive here just now. I came here to see you, listen to you, talk to you, and gain your advice. I was hoping that you would really be able to help me. But I guess I was wrong. I just want you to know, I didn't come here just to get medicine," he said, his voice trembling.

He got up and walked out. My mouth actually dropped open.

What did I just do? If this had been Jesus who had come to see me, would I have treated Him in such an unattentive and dismissive manner? Remorse filled my heart and I ran after the man. "Please, Sir, come back inside." I implored.

"It's O.K." He walked away, tears welling up in his sad eyes.

And there I stood, seeing my true self. Exposed. And who was I? I was the kind of person who would kick Jesus out after a five-hour train ride, three-hour bus ride, and two hours of walking. Disappointment and regret flooded my heart.

During the next morning's prayer meeting, I tearfully confessed to my encounter with the patient. "Jesus called each one of us here to share His love with 'the lesser brothers of mine' with care, kindness, and respect. I've preached on these values so many times, but yesterday I didn't practice them. Dear brothers and sisters, let's remember that our mission is not about buildings, hospitals, or clinics, but, rather, about the people and reaching those people through our loving actions as extensions of Christ, exuding His fragrant love in all situations, at all times. Let's devote ourselves fully to even the smallest tasks according to His will. It's through these seemingly inconsequential opportunities that the greatest fruit will come to bear."

That morning our team repented together as one before the Lord. We thanked Him for giving us the opportunity to see ourselves, our mission, and His will more clearly.

Loving Your Enemy

Learning to bless those who mistreat you is hard. I got into a conflict with one of my mission colleagues. To my utter dismay, I learned that he was spewing cruel and acrimonious rumors about me to anyone who would listen. Nothing seemed to please him. Whatever I did, he condemned. Needless to say, very bad feelings developed between us. Many times I wanted to confront him. More often, I avoided him. Finally, I began to pray about the situation. "Dear Lord, since we're clearly unable to work together, please take him away and allow me to work in peace. He's irritating me to no end!"

Many days passed and I could hear no answer. One day the thought occurred to me, "It's the Lord's work, so why should you be the only one doing it?"

So, I changed my prayer. "Dear Lord, please take either me or him to heaven."

However, asking the Lord to take someone's life, including my own, did not seem right, so I changed my prayer again. "Dear Heavenly Father, please touch his heart with the power of your Holy Spirit and bring about the much needed change necessary in this man."

I had been praying this for about ten days when I heard a voice, "What about you? Have you been touched and changed by my Holy Spirit?"

Jesus commands us to love our enemies. However, instead of putting this into practice, I simply looked to the Lord for an easy way out. I was expecting the Lord to change this man, but the Lord was expecting me to change first.

From then on, whenever I ran into this person, I greeted, embraced, and blessed him. "I love you, my brother. God bless you. Please forgive me."

At first my actions caught him completely off guard, and, understandably, he regarded me with suspicion. Nonetheless, I was consistent and kept blessing him whenever the opportunity arose.

And the most astonishing thing began to occur. His attitude toward me began to change.

This man, whose heart had seemed so cruel and stubborn, began to soften. As Jesus had prescribed, loving my enemies, to my great shock and amazement, was bringing about a vital transformation in those who had intended me harm.

I began to think that this was a scenario applicable to our work in North Korea, as well. If the Lord's loving grace could transform someone like me, I was confident that it could also transform an entire nation like North Korea, one person at a time.

Keeping Warm Hearts in the Cold

I was very surprised when a close friend of mine declared his intention to become a full-time missionary. He was a very successful business man and ran an American company with over four hundred employees. He wanted to give it all up to adopt the meager existence of a missionary, earning little, living off less. It was so unexpected. Up until recently, he had hesitated to even participate on any short-term medical mission trips with us. "I don't know anything about medicine or missions. I doubt if I could be of any help," he would always say.

"You don't have to be a doctor to be part of our short-term medical mission teams. You just need the ability to connect with people in a warm, kind, and loving manner. Are you able to do that? If so, you can definitely be of help," I would encourage him repeatedly.

He finally joined one of our trips. And it was during that trip that he and his wife made the decision to become full-time missionaries. I did not even know that they had been thinking along those lines. Nonetheless, I thanked the Lord for sending us two more wonderful and capable co-workers, but I was also concerned. "Are you sure about this? What about your company?"

"Dr. Park, though we didn't say anything to anyone, my wife and I have been in deep prayer about this for a while. I've enjoyed my business, but, at this point in my life, I'm searching for something different. I want to dedicate the rest of my days to doing the Lord's work. My wife and I both agree that this is the right thing to do."

They sold off their business and enrolled in a missionary school program in Hawaii. Afterward, they joined our SAM mission full time and were immediately sent to work at one of our clinical outposts in "J" city, China. In "J" city, the climate is such that the winter temperatures can drop to a frigid minus forty degrees Celsius, a drastic change from the warm and sunny Los Angeles climate they had enjoyed for over twenty years.

During their first year in "J" city, they sent me the following Christmas card:

Merry Christmas! We've buried all hate, feuds, vindictiveness, and negative things of the world under the white snow. We're drawing new life from the beautiful love of Jesus, our hearts dedicated to SAM.

It's not that we're doing anything remarkable, but we're just humbly dedicating ourselves the best way we can. We give all thanks to our Lord that you're in good health. We also give thanks for the mighty grace of His love and the many SAM supporters. We're praying for continued success in this important medical ministry of love. We're experiencing the warmth of His grace, even in this bitter, cold winter.

It's minus 40 degrees Celsius and we're surrounded by ice, snow, and biting winds. It's difficult to breathe. However, we thank God for giving us the ability to serve Him in this capacity.

We send you our love and blessings.

What a beautiful confession! Having disentangled themselves from the embracing comforts of their former lives, they now possessed nothing, and yet, the Lord's grace had infused their souls with the richness of all men. They lived and served in a region so remote that it was not easily accessible, even by way of modern transportation, and yet, they felt not alone, but instead, surrounded with His holy presence. Despite frigid temperatures, the inextinguishable fire of Almighty God was keeping their hearts warm in the cold.

Another one of our core SAM members is in her late sixties. She manages the SAM-Korea office. Due to her tireless and diligent efforts, SAM-Korea has never encountered any financial difficulties. She rarely relaxes her vigilance in ensuring that not even a single penny is unaccounted for or wasted. Yet, she refuses to accept any monetary compensation for her services. She fully donates of her time and energy.

Her grown daughters constantly plead, "You're working too hard. Why don't you take some time off to travel? You need to enjoy your life!" But she remains steadfast and loyal. She simply smiles and jokingly tells her daughters that she would worry about facing job jeopardy at SAM if she took time off to travel. It is due to the selfless dedication of such incredible people that SAM has developed and expanded into the world-wide, soul-saving organization that it is today.

Our SAM mission is composed of hundreds of brothers and sisters toiling endlessly and faithfully around the world, without much thanks or remuneration. Jesus is their sole source of strength and singular reason for their dedicated service and tearful prayers.

Everything Is Accomplished through His Grace

I taught at the University of California-Davis Medical School in Sacramento. Several times a week I would make the one-and-a-half-hour drive to and from the medical center. Those long-distance, solo commutes worried my wife, especially after an exhausting overseas trip.

However, I always reveled in my time alone on the highway. I could shut off my phone, feel the dizzy, frenetic pace of the world ebb away, and flourish in my own stress-free space. Some days I would listen to sermon tapes. Some days I sang my favorite hymns. At other times I planned my next newspaper column. Mostly, however, I spent time in prayer. Those three hours of solitude became treasured moments of quiet reflection and restorative meditation.

One day as I was driving home after a full day at school, I decided to take an introspective look at myself. People often referred to me as being an accomplished person, full of joy, charisma, and 'an apostle of his time.' I have to admit, I did not exactly dislike or object to hearing myself characterized by such venerable descriptions. Were these accurate?

I had never pondered this before. For a predominant portion of the long drive home, my mind raced back and forth in search of evidence as to why I should deserve to hear such praise. I was almost home when it occurred to me that these high opinions and commendations might have been nothing but empty words. They're all lies, nothing but falsehoods! My heart sank. I knew myself better than anyone else—my encumbrances with arrogance, false pride, stubbornness, shortcomings in love, humility, and prayers. Nonetheless, people thought so highly of me. Why was that? Perhaps, I was simply a good pretender, convincing in my show of faith. Suddenly, I became afraid.

"What a wretched man I am! Who will rescue me from this body of death?" (Romans 7:24).

I was reciting the apostle Paul's confession in my small car, when I heard the Lord speak to me, "It is by God's grace that you've been able to live and work the way you have."

Compliments, praise, glory—everything belongs to Him. I can boast of nothing but for the supreme love of our Lord Jesus Christ. We exist for His glory, not the other way around. Shamefully weak and undeniably human, it must be a challenge for the Lord to use me as one of His instruments. And yet, He has entrusted me with His work. May my digressive shortcomings and stumbling deficits exponentially magnify and more brilliantly radiate the manifestation of His power and absolute perfection.

My grounding anchor and my wings of divine grace, He sees me exposed in the fullness of my attendant shame and chooses to love me still.

To Him be all praise, glory, and honor!

An Unexpected Christmas Gift

Just before Christmas one year, I received a letter that was delivered to me at the Dan Dong Hospital.

Dear Elder Park:

Hallelujah! Thanks and praise be to our God. I am weeping as I write this letter, thinking of you and my past. I received life-changing blessings in meeting you after my desperate escape from North Korea.

Because of your generosity and kindness, I am now a Christian. When I became orphaned after my father was murdered by a fellow North Korean refugee, you reached out to help me, and I'm so truly grateful. Thank you so much for obtaining a residence permit for me to stay here in China and arranging for me to live with deacon "G." I'm in junior high school now and at the top of my class in my studies. I pray and worship every day before school. My happiness has come about because of the Lord, you, and Deacon "G."

I'd like to return to North Korea someday to share the love of Jesus with my people there. I believe that helping to carry on your good work is the best way I can truly thank you for all that you have done for me.

Although we're physically apart, we're all one in the body of Christ. I pray that we'll meet again someday soon.

May God bless you with good health and long life. Please pray for me. Good bye for now. I do hope to see you again soon.

Sungsil Chung
Daughter of our Lord Jesus Christ
December 3, 2000.

I read this letter over and over, and wept as I did so. Sungsil was a teenager, whose young existence had been raped with gruesome tragedy and suffering. This child's indissoluble fortitude and endurance for survival in overcoming heartbreaking circumstances—which would have crippled men and women twice her years—showcased a stunning maturity that far belied her tender young age. Her commitment to one day return to North Korea to share God's love with her people touched my heart. I just knew that the Lord was taking great delight in Sungsil's devotion to Him. I read the letter at the next morning's prayer meeting and during the ensuing Sunday worship service, as part of my testimony.

This letter was a Christmas gift, and what a Christmas season it was turning out to be! It was a season to pray for children like Sungsil. For every child such as Sungsil that we saved, there were hundreds of thousands of children we could not. Locked in a desperate, punishing battle for their very lives, these little ones were barely existing, somewhere along the cold, bleak, and unforgiving banks of the Tumen and Yalu Rivers.

Breaking Out into a Cold Sweat at the Unbong Dam

March 2001. Fifty of us participated on a medical mission trip to Jian, China. Each day hundreds of patients flocked to us from around the Yalu River region, and we worked hard to treat them all.

One day a colleague pulled me aside and whispered, "I've just heard about a group of North Korean timber cutters living near the Unbong Dam. It's about an hour drive from here."

My eyes widened with excitement as he expounded further. "I found a Korean-Chinese taxi driver who can take us there. He's promised me that he can get us past the security checkpoints along the way, so we shouldn't have any problems getting to the North Koreans to help them. If we leave now, we'll make it back before dark."

We quietly pulled aside another colleague to join us and quickly began shoving food and medicine into any available empty boxes. Minutes later we loaded our bulging boxes into a taxi waiting out front and left. As my colleague had stated, we breezed easily through five heavily-armed Chinese security checkpoints before arriving at the huge dam. Somehow the taxi driver had managed to ease us through without the arousal of any suspicion.

Carrying the armloads of supplies we had brought, we began to cross the massive steel bridge that towered over the Yalu River. Without a second thought for the legality of our actions or the risks we were undertaking, our eager eyes were drawn only to the forest of trees that blanketed the North Korean mountainside where the timber cutters were said to be living.

Suddenly, someone tackled our taxi driver to the ground. Chinese police quickly swarmed around us. A police captain strode toward us. "WHAT ARE YOU DOING HERE AND WHO GAVE YOU PERMISSION TO DO THIS?" he roared.

We were immediately taken into custody and detained at the provincial police department. Our passports were confiscated. My colleagues and I could not speak Chinese, therefore, an intense interrogation of our Korean-Chinese taxi driver commenced. We had crossed over into North Korean territory illegally and were in danger of being arrested on espionage charges in connection with the ongoing crisis over a crashed American spy plane.

We sat silently, helpless and uncertain as to the outcome of our fates. I could feel myself breaking out into a cold sweat, struck by the catastrophic absurdity of our naïve actions and the grave situation in which we now found ourselves. Just then, I recalled the jarring incident with the Chinese police over the wooden cross at the Dan Dong Hospital chapel. The Lord had truly sheltered us with His protection at that time. "Lord Jesus, we were just trying to share some food with the starving North Korean people," I whispered. A sensation of His assurance and protection washed over me and my fear subsided.

The captain walked toward me. "Do you speak Korean?" he asked, giving me a hard stare.

"Yes." I felt a measure of relief that he was Korean-Chinese. At least we would be able to converse in Korean.

"If you're an American citizen, why aren't you carrying out your business legally, through proper channels? Why are you engaging in illegal activities crossing the North Korean border?"

I took a deep breath and weighed my answer. "We're so sorry. We made a very bad mistake and didn't realize what we were doing was illegal. We thought this was a tourist area and simply wanted to share some food with fellow Koreans," I stammered.

There was a long heavy pause.

"This is a highly sensitive and restricted area. I'm sure you crossed many security checkpoints to get here, and yet, you thought this was a tourist area?" he asked skeptically. He glanced down at the stethoscope peeking out of my coat pocket and began in a softer voice, "You could have gotten into serious trouble . . . but it appears to me that you are good people with good intentions. If I let you go, you must never do this again. If I catch you next time, I will arrest you."

The captain allowed me and my colleagues to go free, but continued to interrogate our taxi driver further. They took his fingerprints before finally releasing him.

As we made our way back toward our riverside clinic, I leaned forward in my seat and asked the driver, "How did you get us through all those security checkpoints so easily? What did you tell them?"

"They asked me if you were South Koreans or Americans. I said that you were my Korean-Chinese relatives visiting from Yonbian," he replied. "I lied."

We did not share details of our harrowing detour with the rest of our group. There would be no purpose served in announcing our folly to the world. Retrospectively, our impulse action was beyond foolish or reckless, it was dangerous to go dashing off to the dam without proper preparation or thoughtful planning. Caution in accomplishing our work *respectfully* should have been exercised.

The Lord saved us from our own misjudgment and short sightedness, draping us with His kind covering and generosity in the process.

10

The Blessings of a Colleague

March 2001. SAM had over one thousand members worldwide. To propel our organization to a higher level of commitment and action, we decided to launch our first mission conference in San Francisco from May 18-20.

Strategy meetings ensued during which we struggled to brainstorm names of well-known South Korean pastors who could come challenge and encourage us spiritually.

"People say it's easier to invite Jesus to personally show up than it is to catch the attention of a famous Korean pastor," someone joked.

We all laughed. The pastors I knew were so busy that I almost felt sorry to even ask. It would not be easy for any of them to travel all the way to San Francisco to attend a mission conference held by our small organization.

With that said, a list of pastors' names was compiled, and I was given the task of inviting them to our conference as keynote speakers. Before beginning I prayed, "Dear Father, if you would allow just three of these pastors on my list to accept our invitation, I'll know that you're well pleased with our efforts here at SAM."

One of the names was Pastor Il Doh Choi, one of the most renowned pastors in South Korea. I was informed that he happened to be visiting Houston at that time, so I called him.

"Hello Pastor Choi, this is Elder Sai Rok Park."

"Ah, Elder Park, what a coincidence! Actually, I've been carrying your phone number around in my pocket, meaning to get in touch with you. Thanks very much for calling me first. I'm so pleased to talk to you."

Relief washed over me as he recognized my name. I had almost expected him to ask, "Who is Elder Park?"

"I was at a revival in L. A. last week, when a deacon came up to me and suggested that I meet with you," he said.

This is your doing, Lord. Thank you for prearranging and ordering our steps, I thought. I got straight to the point. "SAM is preparing a 2001 mission conference, and I'd like for you to come as one of our special guest speakers."

"Yes, I'd be honored," he said without hesitation. Just like that.

Upon his return to South Korea, he sent me the following confirmation letter:

Shalom!

I'm sorry for the delay in sending you this letter. The construction of our church's charity hospital was once again blocked by the local district office because of complaints from the neighborhood. I haven't been able to sleep for more than four hours a night, and I seem to spend all my time in meetings to resolve this issue. I don't mean to overburden you with this, but I'd ask for your prayers so that we may find a quick resolution to this problem of ours. You're a person of great faith and prayer.

Dear Elder Park, I don't know why you invited a pastor of little faith like me to be one of your speakers. I'm really an unworthy and incapable man, more than you know. Most of all, I'm a sinful man.

There's nothing for me to say except to confess my sins of not being able to love more generously and not being able to carry myself more humbly. I don't know if I'm worthy enough to be a speaker at your conference.

It'd be okay for you to cancel my invitation upon your reconsideration. To tell you the truth, you make me feel very ashamed of myself. Your wholehearted and selfless devotion to sharing the love of Jesus with the poor and destitute people around the world humbles a sinner like me.

I pray for the Lord's mercy.

However, in the event that you don't rescind my invitation, I'll see you at the conference.

Pastor Il Do Choi
South Korea

I was numb with incredulity as I read the letter over and over, stunned by his confession. Here he was, a famous lead pastor of a congregation of thousands in South Korea. He worked tirelessly in the distribution of free meals to hundreds of the homeless on a weekly basis, and his church was in the throes of building a charity hospital for the poor and medically underserved. Yet, he was in failing health and required constant intravenous injections for stamina. I thanked the Lord for arranging this pastor, in particular, to be one of our speakers.

His reference to me as being "a person of great faith and prayer" devoted to "sharing Jesus' love with the poor and destitute people around the world" greatly shamed me. It was I, who was the sinful one. Although I often spoke of loving more unconditionally and living more humbly, I fell short of this time and time again, blocked by my own false sense of heightened self and pride.

Overall, I extended invitations to six renowned South Korean pastors to attend our conference as honored guests. I had thought that having just three acceptances would be an extraordinary blessing. Much to my astonished delight, all six pastors enthusiastically agreed to attend and made themselves available despite extremely hectic schedules.

How wonderfully our cups were overflowing with the goodness and mercy of our Lord.

How Could a North Korean Dove Be So Fat?

Our next task was to advertise and market the SAM 2001 Mission Conference. After much deliberation, a title was agreed on, "Crossing the Rivers to World Missions—North Korean Missions and Global Missions." We needed public relations materials—posters and invitation letters—and it was paramount that we quickly find a capable graphic designer who could help us do so. A task that proved to be much easier said than done. "Sorry, can't help you, I'm tied up with other projects"; "I've never done any design work for a religious event"; "Not interested."

The date of the conference was quickly approaching, and we still had no luck in finding a graphic designer. Virtually, at the last minute, we were introduced to a young designer who did not believe in Jesus, but stated that he did not hold anything against Him either. As we were running out of both time and options, we threw caution to the wind and entrusted this young man with the responsibility of designing for us.

"The theme of the conference emphasizes helping the North Korean people as a way to world missions. By helping the North Korean people out of their current misery and introducing them to Jesus, it's our prayer that they'll someday become powerful evangelists for the entire world," we explained.

Being a non-Christian, his tepid response left us feeling a bit uneasy. However, a few days after our initial meeting, he presented us with a first draft.

His design depicted the Yalu River Bridge (connecting China to North Korea) broken in the middle. Dan Dong, China, was ablaze in dazzling lights. Across the river, Sin Eu Ju, North Korea, was enveloped in darkness. A brilliant light shined from above, and a large dove, representing peace and the Holy Spirit, was soaring triumphantly out of North Korea.

My co-workers were not at all pleased with the design and began asking critical, pointed questions. "Shouldn't the dove be flying from Dan Dong City to North Korea instead of the opposite way? Help is supposed to be going into North Korea, not coming out of there"; "How could a North Korean dove be so fat? There's nothing to eat there."

The designer sat silently, not offering to defend or explain his work in any way. But from the moment I laid eyes on the design, I knew that the work had been done by the Holy Spirit.

"North Korea remains a dark and barren land physically and spiritually. But if the Holy Spirit descends on its people, they'll receive His power and become mighty witnesses for North Korea, and eventually the rest of the world. It's absolutely right for the dove of the Holy Spirit to look powerful. How'd you get this brilliant idea?" I asked.

The young designer shrugged; he did not really know.

But I did. "Have you ever attended church? Are any of your family members Christians?"

"No, my family and I are all Buddhists."

Why We Need to Be One in Him

The day before our SAM 2001 Mission Conference, thrilled anticipation and excitement stirred the air. The collective expenditure of extremely long hours of toiling preparation ensured that the conference events would transpire according to plan. Despite the gallant efforts employed, I began to obsess over the number of attendees. Too small a number would be extremely disappointing, not only for my SAM co-workers, but especially for the six pastors who had cleared their jam-packed schedules and flown in from South Korea to participate with us.

It was almost midnight and I lay in bed, wide awake. Perhaps we had overreached and been too ambitious concerning the agenda for this conference. For Friday we had scheduled a full day from nine in the morning to ten at night. Was it wise to schedule Friday this way, as most people had jobs? Perhaps we should have scheduled only evening sessions.

Just then, the wooden cross at the Dan Dong Hospital chapel came to mind and the Lord spoke to me: "You are to be united as one flock, with none missing." It dawned on me that a requisite expectation for a large number of attendees was an inconsequential detail. Even if only a handful of people attended, we would still experience God's glory in coming together to pray as one heart and one mind, united in Him. Be it ten people or ten thousand people, the Lord would colonize the perfect number of attendants according to His will and for His glory.

Hundreds of people attended.

The Lord in His great mercy filled each day's attendance to maximum capacity. People were greatly blessed by the conference, inspired by the preaching of our six honored guest pastors. Many commended our unity: "We're confident that God delights in SAM. We found it so beautiful to see the collective devotion of all the SAM volunteers united as one in their commitment to the Lord."

Hallelujah! We are all one in the same body of Christ, a rich lineage of sons and daughters, spiritual descendants of the one true king.

A New Luke Writes a New Acts

A great number of people participated in our seventh SAM medical mission trip, which necessitated dividing the team into two separate groups. One team headed to Ussrisk, Russia, while the other traveled to Jian, China. Afterward, our two teams would meet before making the long 750-mile journey back to the Dan Dong Hospital.

I accompanied the medical team headed to Ussrisk. Each day, within minutes after the set up of our field clinics, we would be inundated with two to three hundred patients eagerly flocking around us seeking help.

One morning, as I took a short break from seeing patients, I noticed a large crowd congregating a short distance from our clinic site. I heard shouts of, "Amen!" "Hallelujah!" "It's a miracle!"

We were used to such exclamations; but on that day, these sounded particularly different. One of my colleagues suddenly ran towards me. "It's a miracle! A paralyzed man just stood up!" he shouted.

I immediately followed him to find people in tears and dancing jubilantly.

"It's a miracle! God truly lives!"

That morning, a paralytic patient had been carried into our clinic on someone's back. That same patient had been prayed for and was now jumping and leaping about like a wild deer, in ecstatic tears of joy.

From the corner of my eye, I saw several members of the Russian police silently observe the scene, and then slowly slink away. They always seemed to slip away whenever we Christians became overjoyed by supernatural events. Just two days before, a patient afflicted with blindness for three years, recovered his vision after receiving acupuncture treatment and prayer.

As I watched this once-invalid man excitedly dance and skip around, I recalled the words of a pastor, a close friend of mine whom I dearly loved. After returning from my first trip into North Korea, he had come to see me. I relayed details of all that I had encountered in North Korea, and afterward he tearfully prayed for me—"I want you to become a new Luke who writes a new Acts of our contemporary time," he told me.

Initially, I translated this to mean—"Since you're a doctor, you should strive to walk with Jesus in your life, just as Luke had in his." However, as I continued to experience and witness God's extraordinary miracles, I gained another understanding of these words.

"I tell you the truth, anyone who has faith in me will do what I have been doing. He will do even greater things than these, because I am going to the Father" (John 14:12).

The night of Jesus' arrest, the apostle Peter betrayed Jesus three times, in fear for his life. Peter panicked, forgetting all that he had seen, heard, and witnessed during his time with the Lord. He crumbled under his own human frailty. The Holy Spirit would later descend on him, transforming him into one of the most powerful witnesses for our Lord.

"You will receive power when the Holy Spirit comes on you; and you will be my witnesses in Jerusalem, and in all Judea and Samaria, and to the ends of the earth" (Acts 1:8).

As I embrace the task of devotedly keeping my faith and vigilantly holding to all that I have seen, heard, and witnessed, may the Lord's will be accomplished through me and, sometimes, in spite of me. With the Holy Spirit's guidance, may He transform me to become a new Luke who writes a new Acts for our time.

Amen!

Re-tired (New Tires)

My life was becoming more frantically busy. Almost every week, I found myself traveling to a different continent to preach. I also had my students and patients to see at the University of California-Davis Medical School and the Northern California VA Medical Center, at least three days a week. My calendar was fuller than ever, even more so than when I had my private practice.

Surprisingly, as busy as I was, I could not have been in better health. Since embarking in my work as a medical missionary, I seemed never to be afflicted with illness anymore. Still, I was faced with the realization that adjustments had to be made as my mission activities had simply become too demanding to concurrently maintain my medical school and hospital responsibilities. It would be heart wrenching to leave an environment and discipline in which my entire professional identity and career had been carefully cultivated for over forty years, but I knew that it was time.

I consulted my wife. "I think I'm going to quit my job at the school."

"You should have done it a long time ago," she retorted quickly. That was all the confirmation I needed to confidently move forward with the decision, without reservation.

February 2002. I took an early retirement and stepped down from my posts at both the medical school and the VA Medical Center. As I walked out of the medical school hospital, crossing the street into the sunshine for the very last time, deep gratitude flooded my heart. My career as a physician had been a transformative evolution over four solid decades in a rigorous scientific learning and teaching culture. I would not soon forget: my patients, my colleagues, school deans, sleepless nights delivering babies, the triumphs, the calamities, the day I was selected by interns and residents as the best instructor at the hospital—so many experiences.

I once had to perform surgery on a three-hundred-pound patient at the VA Medical Center, and she almost died during the procedure. This patient had been diagnosed with a large benign tumor in her uterus, but, given her weight, her first doctor had determined that conventional surgery would be too risky. She was referred to me for an endoscopic procedure.

There was no surgical table large enough to accommodate her body size, and two beds were put together for her in the operating room. As the surgery commenced, I proceeded to insert a large endoscope into her abdomen, and as I did so, a fourth-year resident pulled the instrument back, stating that something was strange. Within seconds, blood began rushing everywhere. An artery had been severed; the endoscope must have accidentally cut through it. Immediately, we opened her up. Her abdomen was deep and wide, a pool of blood gushing relentlessly. I could not see anything but a massive, pulsating ocean of red. Two residents and I tried our best to stop the spouting and spurting, to no avail.

We started an immediate blood transfusion. "Her blood pressure is falling fast!" the anesthesiologist yelled. "I don't have a pulse!" he shouted.

Panicked and without being cognizant of even doing so, I began crying out loud to the Lord.

In Korean.

"OH LORD JESUS! PLEASE SAVE THIS WOMAN. EVERYONE KNOWS I'M A MISSIONARY DEVOTED TO SAVING LIVES, BUT IF THIS PATIENT DIES UNDER MY CARE, WHAT WOULD HAPPEN TO YOUR NAME? PLEASE HAVE MERCY ON US. PLEASE SAVE HER LIFE!"

People in the operating room had shocked and gaping expressions on their faces. To them, I was shouting incoherent, crazy gibberish. At that very moment, I yelled, "I got it!" I located the severed artery as if I had caught a small thread in a rushing river. The patient's life was saved.

For some time afterward, word continued to spread like wildfire around the hospital about "Professor Park's crazy, nonsensical talk that saved the patient."

On the day she was discharged, the patient gave me a hug and said, "I know that it was your God that saved me. Thank you!"

Amazing grace.

During my final drive home on that day, I prayed to the Lord, "Dear Father, use me to help save starving and dying souls." I repeated the prayer over and over. When I got home, I announced to my wife, "Honey, I'm not going to retire. I'll just 're-tire,' put on new tires, and race towards God for the rest of my life."

My wife beamed as brightly as the sun.

The Blessed X-Ray Machine

With the news that I had resigned from my teaching position, an investor came to see me. "Given your successful career, would you consider joining me in running a large hospital for profit? I have money ready to invest in such a facility here in Silicon Valley," he said.

Upon hearing the words "making money," I instantly perked up. For some time we had been trying to buy an X-ray machine for the Dan Dong Hospital, without any success. This man's offer to open a for-profit hospital sounded like the perfect remedy to our ailment! Fundraising was exasperatingly difficult. How wonderful it would be to procure monies enough to buy the X-ray machine and cover all expenses necessary to properly support our missionaries without the ubiquitous albatross of financial worries perched over our heads. The investor began searching for an ideal hospital site and hired an architect.

One morning as I read my Bible, the Lord spoke to me. "When did I ever ask you to make money? Has the lack of finances ever hindered you from doing my work?"

Immediately, these words prompted me to reorganize my thoughts. Was I not supposed to pursue this hospital project, after all? I pondered this for a while, feeling confused and uneasy. Eventually, a meeting was scheduled with the investor during which I politely, regretfully, declined his offer. "I'm sorry, but I won't be able to join you in this hospital venture," I told him with fearful reservation.

He was very disappointed. And so was I. I brooded miserably over my decision. Had I made a hasty decision in allowing a once-in-a-lifetime opportunity to slip through my fingers? Was I blowing a God-given chance? Conflicted resentment slowly dismantled my joy and confidence.

A few weeks later, I received a phone call from a good friend of mine I had not seen in a while. "Let's meet for lunch," he suggested.

"I'm afraid that I don't feel like going out."

"Please come," he insisted.

Unable to refuse him any further, I relented and joined him for lunch.

As we finished our meal, I made motions to reach for the bill when he suddenly asked, "How can I really help you? What are you needing most at the Dan Dong Hospital right now?"

"Well . . . we've been trying to acquire an X-ray machine without any success," I said.

"How much would it cost to buy one?"

"One hundred thousand dollars."

"I'll give you the money," he said instantly.

A thought immediately raced through my mind. Darn! Another missed opportunity! I should have asked for $500,000! I regretted saying only $100,000, but then, I had not been expecting to receive any money from him at all.

"For a while, I've been praying for a way to help you, and it's amazing because the figure of $100,000 kept coming to my mind. And now you've just told me that that is exactly the amount that you need; it all makes sense." His face eased into a wide smile. "I'd be most happy to donate the $100,000 for the X-ray machine."

Euphoria flooded my heart! The Lord had made a way and provided, even when it had seemed that there was no way! However, I felt like a thief for even thinking about $500,000. Had I expressed my greedy desire for $500,000, my friend probably would have thought twice about presenting me with his generous gift.

Coming home with the check in my pocket, I went straight to my study and knelt before the Lord in repentance. Once again I was ashamed. My sinful nature had crept through, prompting me to resort to worldly ways to do the Lord's work. Despite my shortcomings, the Father's grace continued to pour forth. Shortly thereafter, several churches and individuals collectively donated more than $500,000 worth of much needed medical equipment for the Dan Dong Hospital.

The X-Ray Machine Weathers a Bad Storm

We wasted no time in buying the X-ray machine. With our reticence and inability to trust the quality of Chinese manufactured machines, we decided to buy one in South Korea and have it shipped to China. We contracted a broker to handle the complicated transaction through customs and waited for the delivery to Dan Dong. Six months later, the machine still had not arrived, and there was no further communication from the broker.

Finally, I contacted the broker and demanded, "Where is our X-ray machine? Do you know how long it's been? Why haven't you delivered it already?"

As a pacifying gesture, she sent some parts of the machine through Chinese customs, but ultimately stated, "I need more money. It's a very difficult process."

Against our better judgment, we provided her with an additional $10,000. Nothing more happened. Our calls and pleadings went unheeded and I became greatly distressed about the waste of our donor's money. I slept fitfully, inundated with bad thoughts and feelings toward the broker.

One evening, I received a call from one of our missionaries from our South Korean office. "Elder Park! I'm at Incheon Harbor. Someone told me about an X-ray machine sitting idle here. I came to check on it, and it turns out, it's ours!"

"What! How can this even be possible?" I asked, stunned. "Is it true?"

"I heard from a fellow passenger on a ship to Incheon that the Korean customs office was about to throw away an abandoned X-ray machine. The machine wasn't even covered. All this time it sat outside exposed to the rain, wind, and elements. I'll try to find a way to ship it to Dan Dong, myself."

Mercifully, we were spared the heartache of an expensive loss. The X-ray machine weathered many bad storms and yet, incurred no damage at all. It remains in good condition, functioning well to this day.

Praise God!

11

Life across the Rivers

After sunset many North Korean women frantically roam the streets of Dan Dong, China, in search of food for their hungry children back home. They do not dare move about during the day for fear of capture by either the Chinese police or North Korean secret agents operating stealthily along those border regions. At night, however, they pound on doors of Chinese home owners to beg for food or to sell their bodies in exchange for money. Most shockingly of all, those same areas are inundated with an alarming number of human traffickers in operation, abducting these roaming women and either selling them as slaves or imprisoning them into a life of forced prostitution. Especially vulnerable are the young girls.

How could this be happening to our own people? There seems to be no end to the unfolding sequence of tragedies. What use is South Korea's great economic prosperity, unmatched technological prowess, and elevated global standing, when our own blood brethren in the North are still suffering? We are only as strong as the least of our brothers and sisters. My heart weeps for the wretched in our very own backyard.

At night, stark contrasts between North Korea and China come shockingly into view along the banks of the Yalu River. Amid frenzied progress, explosive development, and economic growth, Dan Dong, China, has flourished into a thriving city with bright neon lights blazing brilliantly in the dark. Its night-time scene is a dazzling sight to behold.

Just barely a mile across the Yalu River sits Sin Eu Ju, North Korea, enveloped in a silent and eerie blackness. We can only wonder how people are able to live when there is no energy to light or heat even a single home. How do people survive during the winter months as temperatures plunge to a deathly twenty or thirty degrees below zero? China is making such amazing progress; why can we not do the same?

It is agonizing.

We Will Believe in Jesus, Too

I was washing my hands after a long day's work at the Dan Dong Hospital when two strangers came to see me. They had made the dangerous escape across the Yalu River from North Korea. They moved toward me like two dark, shrunken, emaciated ghosts. Their black eyes sank deeply into their shriveled faces. I could hardly believe that they had enough strength to make it across the river, let alone stand.

One of the young men spoke. "We tried to bring dried fish to sell, but some Chinese people stole our fish and now we have nowhere else to go. We've been in hiding all this time and don't know what to do. We can't go back home empty-handed . . . our families are starving. We heard that we could find help from you, and in a last ditch effort, we ran over here in broad daylight."

I saw despair in their teary eyes, misery etched into their weary faces. I took hold of their hands and asked them, "How much would it cost for your families to survive for one year?"

They stated the amount in North Korean currency, and I converted the figure to U.S. dollars. They needed the equivalent of $250 to feed a family of six abundantly for one year. I gave them each the equivalent of $250 in Chinese currency and told them to go and feed their hungry families waiting back home.

Taking the money into their hands, they both suddenly crumpled to the floor, and burst into loud, wailing sobs, pounding the ground with their fists in disbelief. "We were hopeless," they cried. "We couldn't even feed ourselves for one day. But now, suddenly out of nowhere, we have enough money to feed our families for an entire year. How is this possible?"

"Because you are fellow Koreans in need," I told them, "and because I'm a Christian and serve the Lord Jesus Christ."

"Thank you! You saved our lives after a month of hell. Thank you." They grasped my hands tightly as they said goodbye, sobbing uncontrollably. "Dear doctor, we'll believe in Jesus, too."

Hastily brushing away their tears, they walked backwards, exiting my office with their heads held in a low bow. I can still see them vividly in my mind.

Truthfully, the paradoxical challenges and endless complexities of maintaining this mission wears me out, drains me. Too often progress degenerates into futility and we find ourselves unequipped to intervene against the potent assaults of repressive intimidation, oppression, and injustice. The joy of saving one life physically and spiritually becomes eclipsed by the ominous reality of millions of people suspended precipitously over the centripetal black hole of starvation and death. Rethinking the implications of our efforts often leads us to question, Does saving one life carry any real significance, when millions upon millions are still dying? Many times I feel like quitting. And yet, bringing about a transformation in the lives of people such as these two young men, saving one life at a time, populating the kingdom of heaven, one soul at a time, constitutes the very core essence of our mission.

"If a man owns a hundred sheep, and one of them wanders away, will he not leave the ninety-nine on the hills and go look for the one that wandered off? And if he finds it, I tell you the

truth, he is happier about that one sheep than about the ninety-nine that did not wander off. In the same way, your father in heaven is not willing that any of these little ones should be lost."
(Matthew 18: 12 – 14)

Spiritual awakening, even if in only one individual, is the epitome of significance in the eyes of the Lord, and this is what renews my spirit and spurs me on.

I have received numerous letters from those I have had the privilege to help. These letters exude enthusiasm and proud proclamations of newfound faith, "I've memorized the book of Matthew by heart!" or "I've memorized the entire Gospel of Mark!"

Each time I read these letters, I am astonished and so thankful for the Lord's never-ending grace and the humbling privilege of reaching the North Koreans, a people He has claimed for His very own.

I Am a Lone Christian

My colleagues and I made a visit to a Chinese home church (formerly called the underground church). This particular home church was set up in a cramped room of a run-down shanty that looked as if it would collapse with the slightest wind or movement. A roughly hewn small wooden cross hung limply on the right-side wall and a pulpit, comprised of a mid-sized empty box, stood in the corner. On any given night, forty to fifty exhausted refugees would cross the Yalu River from North Korea to frequent this home church in search of food and medicine. There were only seven regular members in this church, with six of the members hailing from the family that owned the home. These people placed their lives at tremendous risk to help the North Korean refugees. Farming small mountainside fields was their only source of income. They could scarcely support themselves, and yet, they were willing to share what little they had with complete strangers in need.

During our visit we encountered several North Korean refugees who had come for help. We had brought supplies with us from the Dan Dong Hospital and provided each refugee with bulging sacks of corn, potatoes, and medicine such as aspirin and antibiotics to take back to their families. Many had crossed the Yalu River from Sin Eu Ju, North Korea.

Observing the frenzied ardor with which the food we had distributed was ravenously devoured, broke my heart. These refugees lived, breathed, and slept with starvation as an unrelenting, torturing companion. I approached an elderly man, the oldest of the refugees. His sun-weathered face was adorned with a thin scraggly white goatee. The strain of his hard life seemed to be rudely carved into numerous deep crevices that patterned across his worn skin. He gnawed hungrily at a potato. "How were you able to come here tonight?" I asked as I sat down beside him.

"I told the North Korean guards that I was visiting relatives in China," he said between bites.

"Are you free to do so? Are you able to come and go as you please?"

He glanced around furtively, leaned over, and whispered in my ear, "I gave them money."

"What do you do when you come here to China?" I asked.

"Well, I usually come here for help, and we study the Bible and receive discipleship training." His voice was barely a whisper, but his demeanor was defiant and strong.

"As a Christian, how do you believe in Jesus in North Korea? Are you able to pray and sing praises together with others?"

"No!" he shook his head emphatically. "I'm a lone Christian there. I pray and sing praises to God, but do it alone. And always quietly. Sometimes I'm able to get together with two or three other people for prayers, but never more than three. Even then, we rotate different people each time. We can't meet with the same people or at the same locations; it's much too dangerous."

"When did you first come to believe in Jesus?"

"When I was a child, before the Korean War. I attended Sunday schools with my mother. But it's Deacon "K," a Korean Chinese who visits North Korea frequently, who has really helped to further my knowledge about the gospel and taught me more about Christ. I'm not afraid to die anymore. My only hope is in Christ." His voice quivered with emotion as his eyes began filling with tears. He put down his potato. "Even with the help we get here, my children and grandchildren are still suffering," he said, as a tear rolled slowly down his cheek.

North Korean Christians are struggling to survive, but their love of the Bible is proving indefatigable. North Korean underground Christians have maintained their faith over the past sixty years under the oppressive burdens of insidious hunger and pandemic diseases. I remain convinced that their dehumanizing entrenchment in the bowels of life is not for naught. The Lord will someday inaugurate these people into powerful, heroic witnesses of the gospel. May the Holy Spirit's healing quickly come and restore the barrenness of their decayed lives, propelling them forward into profoundly empowering transformations of His love. To the poor, suffering, impoverished nations around the world, to people living without hope, may the

Conducting a prayer meeting at an underground church at border

North Korean people's legacy someday be established as one of the most graphic living evidences and astonishing witnesses of the saving grace of our Lord Jesus Christ.

Amen!

Believers in Heaven

It was heartbreaking to listen to the testimony of a North Korean refugee as she testified at a U.S. congressional hearing for the North Korean Human Rights Committee.

She had spent seven years as a political prisoner in one of North Korea's most notorious concentration camps. According to her testimony, approximately two hundred out of the two thousand political prisoners in her camp were classified as "Believers in Heaven." They were subject to extraordinarily brutal torture and punishment in an isolated section of the camp.

The Christian prisoners were forced to live with their eyes fixed to the ground at all times, as the guards prohibited them from looking up toward heaven or God. The official governmental policy was to spare the lives of those who revoked their faith and pledged their full allegiance instead to "the Great Leader." However, very few did so.

She proceeded to tell the committee, "I personally couldn't understand the Christians, why they chose to suffer for their faith and die horrible deaths. They had a way out of the camps, and yet, many of those people chose to die by being boiled alive in huge pots of molten metal."

The woman broke down into tears as she shared details of her life in North Korea and of the harrowing escape she made with her young son. She had left her husband behind and had no knowledge of what had become of him.

I yearn for that day when the Lord liberates the North Korean people. Until such time, may the Lord abide with them ever so closely, draping them with the grace of His everlasting love, covering them with His exquisite hope.

I Will Boast in North Korea

I received the following letter from one of our missionaries working in "J" City:

I've been busy preparing food for the refugees crossing the frozen Yalu River. Right now, I, too, feel frozen in spirit. One of the young refugees I had befriended turned out to be a spy working on behalf of the North Korean police. All this time, he's been helping to capture other refugees.

This refugee was caught by the police during his initial escape from North Korea. He was tortured, then sent to a concentration camp, and barely managed to obtain a release through his uncle's personal recognizance. After being put through a special re-education program, he was sent to China to function as a spy for the North Korean police. For his uncle's sake and safety, he couldn't refuse. What a national tragedy this is!

We sincerely appreciate the donation of those who've sent medicines as their love offerings. However, we still need more. People here are dying from very treatable conditions. A while back, I took in a young North Korean boy with severely stunted growth. He's seventeen. When we found him, he was only four feet and four inches tall. We've been feeding him high-protein supplements and he's grown three inches already, gained a bit of weight, too. We bought him shoes and long johns, but he refuses to wear them. He says that such clothing doesn't exist back home. He wants to save them and take them back with him.

Today, we sent a young refugee woman we'd been helping

back to North Korea. We provided her with warm clothes, antibiotics, vitamins, and an accordion. The accordion was to bribe one of the North Korean soldiers at the border. He had demanded it of her when he initially let her out of the country. Who could possibly make sense of that! It was sad to see her go, but I'm electrified because I sense the heart of Jesus in her. Passing the love of Christ to people just like her epitomizes the very reason why we're all here.

From Missionary "S," Region "J"

The North Korean refugees we have encountered are not at all inclined to accept the gospel at first. As they have sought out our assistance in desperate need of a place to hide and food to eat, they obligingly read the Bible and hesitatingly sing praises with us at our suggestion and gentle encouragement. However, as the refugees begin to delve more deeply into the gospel, time and time again, we see the inexplicable miracle of salvation forge a dramatic spiritual transformation, as the words of the Bible come alive, grip hearts, and the Holy Spirit awakens sleeping souls. This is how many have come to be saved.

Ironically, the refugees are ultimately forced to return to North Korea, not for a desire to do so, but for the reason that there is no other alternative for them. Safe haven or survivability does not exist for North Korean refugees in China. It is illegal to be a North Korean refugee in China, and it is equally dangerous to be associated with one. These people are compelled to return to their wretched homeland.

As an organization, we are equipped with neither wealth nor power. Our small means of outreach through miniscule gestures of kindness are actions exponentially greater and far more generous than these people have ever experienced or known. Sadly, it is never enough. Even so, we will continue to press on, share in their tears and say, "We love you as we love ourselves. Your hunger is my hunger.

Your suffering is my suffering." Limited though our intersecting paths are with most of these refugees, spiritual transformations through the Lord's saving grace occur in even the most fleeting of these encounters.

The fire and passion for the gospel in converted North Korean Christians is nothing short of astounding. Sheltering under our care, some of the converted refugees have read the New Testament a hundred times, with one refugee having read it almost a thousand times. As detestable as it is to do so, we encourage each to return to North Korea. "Go back to your hometown and share the Good News with others. You're the trumpeters of the gospel and you'll give your fellow countrymen hope to cling to. Through the love of Jesus Christ, you'll impart a message of great joy that can never be taken away."

They return, sharing the gospel with relatives, friends, and neighbors. Many of these refugees continue to risk their lives in making the treacherous journey back into China again to see us when they desire further help and discipleship training. The roots of our North Korean missions are finally deepening!

Blood Is Thicker Than Water

We were on our way to conduct a medical mission in Jang Baek. As we drove up Paek Tu Mountain in a Jeep, three Chinese policemen standing off to the side of the road motioned for us to stop our car. They wanted a ride, and we obliged.

As our car bucked and surged up the mountain road, one of the policemen suddenly yelled, "STOP THE CAR!" Our driver quickly pulled over, and all three of them leaped out of the Jeep, sprinting wildly down a steep slope, as if they were lions on a hungry chase after prey. They had spotted a young North Korean boy trying to cross the border into China. The three policemen quickly surrounded the boy, undid their belts and began whipping and beating him savagely. One of them, however, was lashing him more fiercely than the others. He pummeled the boy viciously with his fists and mustered all his strength in kicking and stomping on the screaming lad with his heavy black military boots. The boy thrashed and rolled around on the ground, crying out and begging for mercy.

How can he be so cruel? He's beating the boy as if he was a wild animal, I thought as I watched helplessly. We had no choice but to continue on our way up Paek Tu Mountain, feeling very badly about the young boy all day long.

Later that same evening, as we descended the mountain, we encountered the same three policemen. Once again they wanted a ride, and again we obliged. As coolly and casually as I could, I asked the policeman who had been particularly ruthless to the North Korean youth, "What happened to the refugee boy from this morning?"

"I'm a Korean Chinese. We just released him and let him go back to North Korea."

I was stunned by his frank confession.

This policeman's treatment of the boy had been very deliberate and calculated; he knew exactly what he had been doing. He had beaten the boy more brutally than his Chinese counterparts and, in doing so, convinced them to turn the boy loose back to the other side of the border instead of officially detaining him. Had the boy been detained according to Chinese law, he would have been turned over to North Korean soldiers, which would have resulted in very severe repercussions, torture, and persecution. Most likely, by persuading his fellow Chinese officers that he had been beaten enough, the Korean Chinese officer was able to spare the boy more punishment and actually spare the boy's life.

In a tragic, ironic twist of fate, the Korean-Chinese officer ended up doing the fellow Korean boy a great favor by the only means available to him—by almost beating him to death. This was a strange way of showing camaraderie for his fellow Korean. Nonetheless, this was probably the best he could do for the poor lad under the circumstances.

Celebrating the Dan Dong Hospital Opening, Once Again

"The opening ceremony in 2000 wasn't a formal one. It was just an informal 'religious event' of yours not recognized by the Chinese government. You need to hold a formal Chinese opening ceremony for the hospital." The Chinese officials relentlessly bullied us with this request for two years. We could see no resolution to the matter other than to reluctantly acquiesce to their nonsensical demand to hold another opening ceremony for the Dan Dong Hospital. Therefore, on October 10, 2003, three years after our original opening ceremony, we conducted a second opening ceremony.

It rained heavily for several days, right up to the morning of the ceremony, as if all of heaven sympathized with our burgeoning disapproval regarding the reproachful manner in which the Chinese authorities conducted their business. To complicate matters, the Chinese authorities suddenly notified us the night before that they would not permit the ceremony that they had imposed on us in the first place.

We were taken aback by the abrupt change in plans by the contravening Chinese authorities. In spite of their newly formed opposition, there would be no way to prevent the ceremony from occurring, as foreign guests and international dignitaries had already arrived and extensive preparations had been made. At the very last minute, a colleague and I, somehow, managed to negotiate a mollifying resolution with the Chinese authorities.

Just prior to the start in the afternoon, the rain suddenly abated. The air remained chilly, but the gloomy clouds that had shrouded the sky all morning dissolved into a grayish blue by the time the ceremony commenced. Forty guests had arrived from the U.S. and South Korea, and a vice consul from the American Consulate in Shen Yang was also in attendance.

"The Dan Dong Hospital has now been officially approved. This is the beginning. I'd like to express my deepest thanks to each and every volunteer and supporter. Heaven works miracles through all of you here at the hospital," I stated to the audience in my welcoming speech.

The opening ceremony turned out to be an unprecedented success with almost one hundred high-ranking Chinese government officials in attendance. This surprised even those Chinese intelligence officials perennially suspicious of our mission.

Just as the ceremony ended, almost as if on cue, the sky once again became a shadowy, brooding gray, spilling forth a pelting rain.

Returning to North Korea after Seven Years

In the winter months the Yalu River freezes over, which allows escaping North Koreans to cross the ice slicked river more easily into China. Sometimes, we could actually see them coming across shivering, dressed in thin clothing, and worn-out shoes, painfully exposed to the cold.

Some of our SAM supporters who ran businesses in the clothing manufacturing and wholesales industries began donating surplus winter clothing to us. We, in turn, would give these to our North Korean refugee patients and to Korean-Chinese people able to travel into North Korea to distribute the clothing there.

Upon receipt of the heavy winter clothes, our refugee patients would often become giddy with delight, as if exuberant children receiving Christmas gifts. They were amazed that clothes could be so thick and warm! Such elated reactions motivated us to think of ways of making more warm clothing available to not only the refugees who directly sought out our help but also to a broader segment of the North Korean population. It became our desire to help these people survive the brutally frigid and long winters.

The effort resulted in our "$25 Campaign to Help North Koreans Survive the Winter." Twenty-five dollars would save one North Korean from starvation, illness, and cold during the winter season from November to March. Of the twenty-five dollars, two dollars would allow us to buy vitamins and antibiotics, and another two dollars would provide a box of instant noodles for one person for an entire month. To sustain a person for five months would cost just twenty dollars.

We negotiated a generous agreement with a South Korean clothing manufacturing company that enabled us to purchase heavily lined winter jackets retailing regularly at seventy dollars, for only five dollars each. Our goal was to make this twenty-five dollars winter survival package available for ten thousand North Koreans. Twenty-five dollars would literally make the difference between life and death.

As we launched the campaign, we encountered much skepticism and dissent: "You'd better not start it because of the way things are nowadays." North Korea's proliferation of nuclear weaponry and erratic missile launches, against the heated protestations of an increasingly wary international community, propagated great reluctance for provision of humanitarian aid and assistance to North Korea. We remained completely unfazed and focused intently, instead, on the need. Political volatility and fractured diplomacy set aside, our brothers and sisters across the border were freezing to death, with no means available to cope—no heat in homes, no winter clothing, no running water, no food.

Six weeks of intense campaigning, resulted in contributions of $380,000, half in cash and the rest through in-kind donations. American pharmaceutical companies made contributions that amounted to over $1,490,000.

The following letter is from a contributor to the campaign:

Hallelujah! I send this love offering to you in the name of our Lord Jesus. I've long been praying for an opportunity like this, and I thank God for allowing me to present it to you on my eightieth birthday. I hope and trust that this love offering of mine will help save one hundred North Korean brothers and sisters in the name of Jesus. Although it's not a large sum of money, I've saved what I could. As I offer this small expression of my faith, I pray that the Lord's glory be revealed in all of this.

Months of negotiations ensued with the North Korean government. We offered our donation of the winter survival items on the express condition that SAM would undertake sole responsibility for the direct distribution of the goods to the general population, to which they assented. In fact, North Korean officials repeatedly assured us of their commitment to fully respect and uphold our mutual agreement. Before our SAM team's departure for Pyong Yang, four twenty-ton trucks were loaded with ten thousand heavy winter jackets embossed with the SAM logo. Also included were the other basic necessities for the survival package, such as vitamins, antibiotics, sugar, corn oil, and instant noodles. The goods were then transported from our Dan Dong Hospital to Pyong Yang via the Yalu River Bridge.

January 20, 2004. My fellow SAM colleagues and I flew into Pyong Yang. I was returning to the country for the first time in seven years since the 1997 banishment order. Unsurprisingly, immediately upon our landing at Pyong Yang Airport, we were ushered into a frightening scene of contention. North Korean customs officials confiscated my passport and accused me of violating the banishment order. "How dare you come back here when you're still forbidden to enter North Korea!"

Heated exchanges erupted between those government officials who had officially invited me back and the customs officials who were now barring me from entering the country. A ferocious argument transgressed to rough haggling and angry shouting between the two groups. Eventually, the hostile friction between the warring officials subsided to an uneasy silence under which lurked a repressed, tangible tension. My passport was eventually returned to me and I was granted a pass through customs. My colleagues and I, however, were badly shaken by the overt, acrimonious display, and we remained on edge with feelings of non-stop anxiety dominating throughout our four-day stay.

We were permitted to directly deliver many of the winter survival goods to Pyong Yang residents and also to the patients at the Pyong Yang Third Hospital. My heart overflowed with joy for the opportunity to visit this facility once again, a facility I had thought I would never set eyes on after my expulsion. Ten years of my life had been devoted to the construction, equipping, prayers, and tears for this hospital.

Feelings of thrilled anticipation and warm nostalgia of returning to the Pyong Yang Third Hospital dissolved the moment I stepped foot inside. Though the hospital structure was relatively new, the building seemed to have fallen into a state of disuse and disrepair. The hallways were shrouded in darkness, the walls, peeling and fading, and the air was shockingly cold. The temperature outside was a chilly minus four degrees Fahrenheit and yet, the hospital provided no heat. Plastic drop cloths hung flaccidly from the ceilings, loosely covering each hallway entrance in a cavalier gesture to prevent icy wind drafts from blowing into patients' rooms. Elderly patients recuperating from recent surgeries rested on the beds we had sent over ten years ago. They feebly held out their hands to thank us as we greeted them. My heart broke as I grasped frozen fingers as cold as small blocks of ice. I wish I hadn't come back. We'd have been better off not seeing this! I thought grimly.

Any hope of overseeing the distribution to completion was crushed by the North Korean government's sudden decision to halt all of our activities. We personally distributed only half of the survival goods we had sent in, which was contrary to our initial agreement. Forced to leave the other half of the goods behind, we fought, we insisted, we strove bitterly to change the minds of the vagarious North Korean officials over the original terms of our distribution agreement. They reluctantly consented to having us return on February 1 to check and confirm the manner in which the remaining goods had been distributed after our departure.

January 29, 2004. A phone call came to me at the Dan Dong Hospital. It was a North Korean government official informing me of the government's decision to place a ten-day moratorium on our team's re-entry date. Anger began to stir inside me. "LOOK, YOU MAY HAVE THE HABIT OF POSTPONING THINGS AT YOUR SLIGHTEST WHIM, BUT WE'RE NOT GOING TO WAIT AROUND ANY LONGER FOR YOUR ARBITRARY DECISIONS. HOW CAN YOU CALL OFF A SCHEDULED VISIT LIKE THIS?" I screamed. Perhaps the truth that I had been too keen to ignore was that any potentiality to truly help a country as collusive as North Korea was nothing more than an idyllic notion, at best, and could never be actualized. Once again, I found myself deeply regretting the outcome. Dispirited, I gave the North Korean official my final edict, "From now on, I won't ever visit North Korea when you people want me to, but when I want to!"

It appeared as if the North Korean government would never concede to any of our demands. Then suddenly, they relented and allowed one SAM representative back into the country to return to Pyong Yang. He was given assurances regarding the distribution of the remaining goods, collecting photographs and receipts as proof.

Although the ability to finish the distribution ourselves had been abruptly suspended, we still had managed to personally deliver the survival goods to many of the suffering citizens. Moreover, we had verification that the goods did not make their way onto the notorious Chinese black market or misappropriated to the North Korean military. In a radical departure from our previous experiences, we had been able to remain fiercely insistent and strong in our dealings with the North Korean authorities. This new critical development was made possible by the existence of the Dan Dong Hospital, our mission base established firmly a mile from the North Korean shores.

One our of trucks full of food and winter clothing crossing the Yalu River Bridge into North Korea

I Memorized the Entire Gospel of Matthew

"Dear Doctor, please save my life. I was told that you could help me," a young woman's small, fragile voice quivered desperately over the phone.

"Where are you?" I asked.

She was in a nearby village, and I left immediately to see her. She was a tiny, frail woman lying violently ill on a soiled cot. After examining her, I determined that she was suffering from an advanced case of venereal disease. She ran a high fever and her belly was enormously inflated, full of infection.

She explained her sad predicament: "I came here to earn money for my family in North Korea. As hard as it was, I left my husband and child behind, and for two years I worked like crazy, sending all the money I earned back home. But a few months ago, I heard that he moved in with another woman from our village. My heart broke when I heard this news and I decided to return to North Korea. Since I couldn't physically cross the rough mountains by myself, I joined three male refugees returning like me. We hid ourselves during the day and crossed the mountains by night. The problem was that these three men would overpower me and rape me whenever they wanted. I went through hell—thirty days of real hell."

My eyes burned with tears as I listened to her relay her brutal and terrifying ordeal. Her infection was so far gone that I honestly did not have any hope that she would survive. I used what is known as triple therapy—a combination of three strong antibiotics—to treat her. To my utter amazement, she recovered almost immediately as she had never before been exposed to such medicines as antibiotics.

As she quickly regained her health and strength, I began sharing the gospel with her. By the time she fully recovered, she had already memorized the entire book of Matthew. She had come out of North Korea distressed, hungrily searching for survival, and alone. She returned, girded with hope, brimming with joy, and her shining face emanating His holy radiance and peace.

I was so grateful for the opportunity to meet her. Saving such suffering, helpless, and rejected souls is the Dan Dong Hospital's mission and sole purpose for existence.

We Bought a New Home in Heaven

I flew back to the U.S. from Dan Dong to embark on a U.S. speaking tour. I was scheduled to share my testimony in a different city each week. Starting out in Portland, my wife and I then headed to Los Angeles, from there to St. Louis before wrapping up in Los Angeles again.

On my last Sunday in Los Angeles, I spoke at three morning worship services at the Logos Church, and then in the late afternoon, I huddled in meetings with staff members from the SAM-Los Angeles branch office. We spent much time in prayer and endless strategizing for a solution to our problems with strapped finances.

The following morning, my wife and I made our way to Los Angeles International Airport to finally return home. We were both physically and mentally exhausted and in much need of restorative rest and solitude. As we waited to board our flight, my cell phone rang. It was a woman who identified herself as Elder Park. She had heard me speak the day before at one of the worship services at the Logos Church.

"I'd like to meet with you."

"Oh, I'm at the airport." I said hesitatingly.

"May I see you there?"

"I'd be so grateful if you could."

She arrived a half hour later. As we shook hands, she thanked me profusely for my testimony. She then proceeded to hand me a small white envelope.

"My daughter and I prayed all throughout the night and have decided that we want to give this to you as our love offering. We were going to use this money as a down payment to buy ourselves a new home . . . we'd rather give this to your mission."

Her eyes filled with tears as she handed me what was apparently a large check. Her hands trembled, as did mine in accepting the check. At that very moment, the concerned faces of my SAM-Los Angeles co-workers flashed in my mind.

"Thank you," I gasped, overwhelmed by her tremendous generosity.

She replied through a teary smile. "We're the ones who should thank you. Thank you for giving us the opportunity to be blessed and challenged by your mission."

Their expression of love and sacrifice for the Lord blessed my soul immensely and imbued my exhausted mind and body with refreshed lightness.

As I leaned back in my plane seat, waiting for the aircraft to take off, I whispered a fervent prayer: "Thank you, Heavenly Father, for being the almighty God of love who always provides. I pray that you'll abundantly bless Elder Park and her daughter, who bought a new home in heaven instead of here on earth."

"Come to Me All You Who Are Weary and Burdened"

April 22, 2004. A devastating train explosion occurred in Yong Chon, North Korea, near the Chinese-North Korean border. The blast, reportedly resulting from a collision between two trains carrying gasoline and liquefied petroleum, instantly killed over one hundred fifty people and wounded as many as eight thousand. The distance between Yong Chon, North Korea, and Dan Dong, China, can be easily traveled by car in one hour. A tide of international media assembled at Dan Dong, hoping to garner news on the incident, as the sealed North Korean borders offered no hint of information. The North Korean government proceeded to declare a state of emergency, and then clamped down on all forms of communication into and out of the country. An action that many experts translated as being an attempt to inhibit foreign reporting and prevent the leak of unfavorable news of the explosion to its own population.

At the Dan Dong Hospital, we rapidly mobilized into action, loading two twenty-ton trucks with all the emergency food and medicines in our possession, in addition to items we quickly purchased on the Chinese market. Under the scrutinizing, steely eyes of the North Korean military, our trucks crossed the towering Yalu River Bridge into North Korea. As we had been able to quickly gather necessary materials from our Dan Dong Hospital, we were the first international organization to respond to the tragedy,

A month later, an urgent call came to me from a North Korean official requesting further assistance from our organization. We wasted no time in responding by quickly loading two train boxcars full of flour and sending them on to Yong Chon. Twelve twenty-ton trucks were then loaded with cement and construction materials. As the trucks were being filled, we risked taking photographs for our own documentation and as updates to our sponsors and donors. We did so stealthily, as the Chinese border police closely monitored our activities with blatant suspicion. In fact, the day before, they had confiscated some of our cameras and destroyed pictures taken of earlier truckloads of relief materials.

Concurrent with the delivery of our relief materials, four SAM members and I were granted permission to enter North Korea via the Yalu River Bridge. With our cavalcade of trucks fully loaded, we began our slow sojourn, trekking across the massive bridge from China. In all the years I had traveled into North Korea, I had always done so by plane. I had never entered by way of the bridge. To surreptitiously record the momentous event, one of my SAM colleagues concealed a small video camera inside his coat pocket.

When I had an opportunity to view the video at a later date, the voice of the covert cameramen could be heard choking back tears as we crossed the bridge, praying, "Oh, thank you, Lord!" Had he been caught, all five of us would have been arrested. Oppressive hegemony heavily permeates throughout that volatile and restrictive region of the world, thickly seeping into every aspect of people's lives. Someone is always watching, following, listening, always a shadow of a menacing presence lurking nearby. The most innocuous actions, even gestures of goodwill and kindness, are often regarded with suspicion. Sometimes it seems necessary to obtain government permission to even breathe the air!

Within twenty minutes of our departure from Dan Dong, we arrived at Sin Eu Ju, North Korea We were greeted with great fanfare by the Vice Chairman of the North Pyong Yang Provincial Committee for Emergency Situations. "The Dan Dong Hospital's initial shipment of emergency medicine last April was the first assistance we received from any international organization. They were put to good use at our hospitals. We're so grateful," he said as he emphatically shook our hands.

We were the only civilian international aid organization given access to the actual explosion site. Observing the sheer magnitude of the destruction left us utterly speechless and stunned. We stood in the center of an overwhelming mass of ruin, with buildings for a three-block radius completely flattened to rubble. The windows of buildings from as far away as half a mile were shattered or blown out. The explosion had occurred between noon and one in the afternoon, as local elementary school children were getting out of school and walking home. An ominous avalanche of abandoned children's school bags had been gathered, indicating that many children had been among the casualties.

Twelve thousand workers had been drafted from around the country to aid in the reconstruction of the explosion site, but the process had been halted by the lack of construction materials. They had waited anxiously for the arrival of our materials. Time was crucial; it was essential to quickly rebuild homes before the onset of winter. Within minutes of our trucks' arrival to the site, dozens of people swarmed around us, swiftly unloading the materials. Surveying the sad, haunted scene of devastation, I watched groups of withered-looking women lugging heavy bags of cement. By the roadside, a gathering of gaunt and haggard-looking workmen sat somberly, barely holding up their heads.

During our stay, the government granted us clearance to visit the Sin Eu Ju Provincial Children's Hospital, where two hundred fifty children were recuperating from injuries related to the explosion. It had been a month since the blast had occurred, and yet, many of the children were still in shock. Many had undergone surgeries to stitch deep and gaping wounds. Others had lost eyesight; some had lost hearing; many had had limbs amputated. The most disturbing factor of this visit was that none of these North Korean children articulated their pain, cried out, or complained despite their great suffering. There was not so much as a whimper or a spontaneous movement. Their eyes simply followed us with blank and hauntingly deadened stares as we walked from bed to bed. Greeting each child, their faces remained expressionless and eerily devoid of emotion. On their chests hung small signs with the imperious slogan:

"I AM AN OBEDIENT CHILD TO THE DEAR LEADER."

What good did we really do? How much help did our few hundred bags of cement and flour really provide? How could we possibly save these children, these people? The futility of our assistance and the insurmountability of the challenges before us left me feeling exasperated to the point of defeat.

"Come to me, all you who are weary and burdened, and I will give you rest" (Matthew 11:28).

I became more resolute that the fundamental solution to ending the systemic, malignant corrosiveness of mindless, mass ideology was for these people to know Jesus Christ and to have the gospel in their lives. Ah! We must press on. Discipleship training must become our top priority!

Surveying devastation of the explosion site at Yong Chon, North Korea.

12

Doctor's Bag Full of Love

Everyday, following my return home, I continued to relive the haunting details of my heartbreaking visit to the Yong Chon explosion site. In the face of so many casualties and catastrophic injuries, the North Korean doctors were incapable of providing any of their patients with sufficient care, as the hospitals and clinics were virtually devoid of even the most basic medicines and supplies.

Sixty years ago, North Korea became a sovereign nation founded on the principle of creating the greatest socialist republic on earth. Two fundamentals that supposedly demonstrated this philosophy were the free distribution system and the free medical care system. In an attempt to implement these ideals, the North Korean government set up free clinics with trained medical personnel in each village of each province throughout the entire country—five thousand clinics in all. However, this system failed miserably, as the clinics became barely functioning, impoverished ghettos, chronically lacking the most basic medicine, supplies, and equipment. The doctors—only rudimentarily trained—were powerless to treat even the most basic and common diseases. According to the World Health Organization's last available figures, North Korea spent less on healthcare than any other country in the world.

Over the years, we had done our utmost to help counter this void by shipping medicines and equipment, to no noticeable effect.

We began praying for an avenue through which we could reach *every* North Korean citizen, for each person to have, in the very least, access to basic medical care.

As I continued to pray about this, the remembrance of a scene I had witnessed long ago in my youth came to mind. It was of a doctor riding a bicycle on his way to visit a patient in a remote rural village. In my mind's eye, I could still see him pedaling along the side of the dirt road, grasping the handle bars with one hand and his doctor's bag firmly clutched in the other. This had left an indelible impression on me as being an embodiment of compassion and a powerful, loving gesture of goodwill.

It suddenly occurred to me that caring for poor patients in remote areas required a doctor's bag full of medicine and love. Excitedly, I exclaimed, "Let's make a doctor's bag of love!" If we were able to pack the doctor's bags full of essential medical goods for each clinic in North Korea, it would be comparable to making doctor's visits with loving hearts!

The next question became, What should we put in the doctor's bag? I wrote out a preliminary list: paracetamols, antibiotics, analgesics, antacids, laxatives, cough medicines, anti-diarrhea medication, bandages, gauze, alcohol wipes, antiseptics, tongue depressors, antibiotic cream, thermometers, stethoscopes, pocket diagnostic sets, scissors, tweezers, syringes, and needles. Someone could administer basic emergency care with these supplies.

I shared my idea with fellow SAM colleagues and with their unanimous approval we immediately put the project into action. We determined that a total of $500,000 would be needed to execute our plan. Sold separately, the entire contents of one bag would cost approximately $200. Inevitably we would have to buy some of the items, but we were optimistic about our ability to acquire donations for most. Thus, we estimated that we would be able to create one fully equipped doctor's bag for only $50. The contents of each bag would allow doctors at the North Korean clinics to treat up to three hundred patients with primary emergency care. Our goal was to send ten thousand of these bags to the five thousand clinics throughout all of North Korea, two for each clinic. The official name for our doctor's bag of love became the Medical Emergency Supply Kit (MESK).

We corralled support throughout the U.S. and South Korea through an intensive fundraising campaign, quickly raising the monies necessary to begin procuring medicines and materials. Most of the medicines and supplies were obtainable in the U.S. Some equipment, such as thermometers, came from South Korea and China, while other supplies came from Taiwan. My wife designed the doctor's bags, and Deacon In Hwan Sohn from our SAM-Korea office manufactured them at his clothing plant in China.

Over four hundred thousand separate items went into creating ten thousand fully equipped MESKs. An agreement reached with the North Korean government allowed us to ship the four hundred thousand items directly into Sin Eu Ju, North Korea. Our MESK supplies came in from different parts of the globe and were stored at a designated warehouse, where they would eventually be packed and assembled into the doctor's bags. The entire process felt akin to a well-coordinated secret operation from a *Mission Impossible* film!

December 6, 2004. Ten SAM members left our Dan Dong Hospital for Sin Eu Ju, North Korea, to oversee the final assembly of the MESKs. I remained in the U.S. at the time. Earlier in the day, I had received news that it had snowed heavily in the Yalu River region. I became fraught with worry for my colleagues who were having to work in a warehouse with no heat in subzero degree weather, with warm water available to them for only thirty minutes each day.

It was one o' clock in the morning when my phone suddenly rang. I was jolted awake from an uneasy sleep. It was the SAM-Korea office. "We just received a phone call from North Korea."

I bolted out of bed. "Is everyone O.K.?"

"Yes, everyone's safe." Relief washed over me.

"However, we've got a problem. Some of the medical supplies apparently didn't make it into Sin Eu Ju. Since the team's not able to delay the packing of the MESK, they're going to try to buy the missing items in China within a day or two. It'll cost us an additional $10,000."

"How much money do we have available right now?" I asked apprehensively.

"About $7,500."

I hung up the phone and turned to my wife. After briefing her, we joined hands and began to pray. With no ability to overcome this hurdle on our own, as miniscule as it seemed, the rest of the night became sleepless for us as we fitfully tossed and turned, our hearts longing for the Lord's provisional answer.

And He provided. Mightily.

Early the next morning, a fax arrived from an evangelist in Texas. He had read one of my books and was deeply moved by our efforts. He had been praying for a way to help us and felt led to donate to our mission. He wrote that he was immediately sending me a check for $2,500.

Hallelujah! The Lord prepared the way, ordered our steps, and navigated us precisely through our obstacle. A few days later, our team in Sin Eu Ju, North Korea, was able to successfully complete the gargantuan task of overseeing the packing, assembly, and distribution of the ten thousand MESKs.

The following account was written by one of the SAM team members:

> For ten days, we worked in frigidly cold weather with no heat and packed 10,000 MESKs with the help of twenty North Korean laborers. When we had finished packing 1,000 bags, we were shocked by the enormity of the heaping mass before us. I couldn't even imagine how large that pile would become when 10,000 bags were finished.

Heavy snow fell from the first day of our arrival. Up until the eighth day of our stay, even the main roads in downtown Sin Eu Ju remained icy and dangerous. However, we remained firm with the North Korean officials, insisting that we had to personally participate in the distribution of the bags in order to confirm their delivery to the clinics.

Here are some of the clinics we delivered to: two MESKs were delivered to the Ryusang District General Clinic in South Sin Eu Ju (its population is 30,000 with sixty doctors and nurses). We then delivered two MESKs to the Namsang District General Clinic in central Sin Eu Ju (its population is 20,000 with fifty doctors and nurses). The following day, as the road conditions improved somewhat, we traveled outside Sin Eu Ju and delivered two bags each to the Euiju Village Farm Clinic (its population is 1,200 with three doctors and five nurses) and to the Daesan Village People's Hospital (its population is 1,500 with four doctors and one nurse).

The clinic doctors were all so pleased by the gift of the MESKs and expressed much thanks. After carefully examining the contents of a MESK, one North Korean doctor stated elatedly, "After treating patients at the clinic in the morning, we try to pay home visits to chronically ill or emergency patients in the afternoon. These medical bags are very much needed and will be put to good use. Thank you."

As heartwarming as it was to know that these MESKs would save many lives, the need in North Korea is so enormous that for some provinces the provision of the MESKs will not be sufficient. Some doctors stated that their clinics were in desperate need of additional basic supplies such as scalpels, needles, and thread. In particular, the words of the head doctor at one of the clinics in Sin Eu Ju, struck my heart. "I'm so grateful for these medicine and medical supplies. But because we have so many thousands of ill patients and we have so little medicine and supplies available to us, the contents of these doctor's bags will not last us more than ten days." I can still see his sad eyes in my mind.

We asked the North Korean Public Health officials to allow us the ability to refill the bags as necessary with new medical supplies. We also asked the officials to permit some of our SAM members to remain behind to ensure proper administration and distribution of the MESKs.

It seems impossible and incredibly miraculous to me that we began this project only *nine weeks ago*, and yet, we have now distributed 10,000 MESK bags to thousands of clinics throughout North Korea. It indeed felt like a *Mission Impossible* operation. Our team felt such joy as we pondered the delight of our Lord, as countless lives and souls would be saved through this project.

Before our team left North Korea, we prayed special blessings over the bags. Only the Lord's mighty hand will break through this frozen land. I'm so thankful for the privilege of having been used by the Lord for this purpose. Missionary "A"

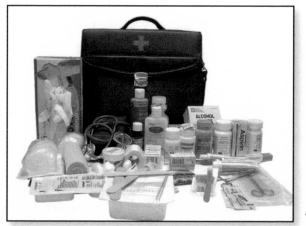

The MESK

Since the original distribution of the ten thousand MESKs in December of 2004, we have transported many more shipping containers full of medical products, supplies, and medicine. On one occasion, with assistance from the North Korean military, we distributed the items directly to the North Korean clinics via helicopter. The MESK project continues to this day, as we faithfully endeavor to reach one more person, in our quest to save lives and save souls.

Refill, a Sure Thing!

We wasted no time in mobilizing a refill campaign for the MESK project.

It was early spring, and the sun's golden morning light inched above the hills to the east, creeping slowly through the window to spill its warmth into our tiny residence at the Dan Dong Hospital. My wife and I were in the middle of our morning devotionals together, praying and praising the Lord, when the phone rang. It was Chairman Hahn from the U.S., a dear brother in Christ and a generous supporter to our mission.

"Chairman Hahn, how are you?" I asked, cheerfully.

"Dr. Park, please help me!" his pleading, desperate voice came feebly through the phone. I was shocked to hear him asking for my help. It was usually the other way around, with me appealing to him for help.

"I've just been diagnosed with prostate cancer. What should I do?" he asked in a trembling voice, full of panic.

"What tests have you taken? Who's your doctor?"

"Based on my PSA test results and a preliminary physical exam, my doctor seems sure that it's cancer."

"Let's not jump to conclusions. Let's have the tests done again. You should also have a biopsy done as well. It could just be an infection. Don't worry. Even if it proves to be cancer, if caught early, prostate cancer is relatively easy to treat and cure. If necessary, I'll fly back to be with you," I assured him.

"Thanks so much . . . I feel better after talking to you."

I placed a call to a good friend in the U.S., who was also a prostate cancer specialist. I informed him of a new patient referral and advised him to prepare for surgery, if necessary.

Three days later, Chairman Hahn called me again. "Hallelujah! The Lord has saved my life. A biopsy proved that it was just an infection!" His voice boomed excitedly over the phone. I felt as much joy and relief in hearing the news as he did!

"Chairman Hahn, let's renew our commitment to living according to the will of our Lord who truly loves us and oversees all things in our lives," I said.

"Certainly! The moment I was told that I might have cancer, all I could think about was my dear wife. Then, my next thought was how much I envied you and your life. I'd like to follow in your footsteps from now on, in full commitment and service to the Lord."

His statement surprised me, and I found myself at a momentary loss for words.

"Dr. Park, how's the MESK project coming along?"

Chairman Hahn sent me a very large check as a love offering in support of the MESK refill campaign. Particularly astonishing about this gift was that the amount exactly covered, down to the penny, the cost necessary to complete the refill project.

It is our goal to refill the contents of the MESK bags at least twice a year, in addition to replacing the old bags with new doctor's bags, once every two years. Through this MESK project may the transformative love, healing, and sustaining power of our Lord Jesus Christ touch the hearts, minds, and souls of each person treated.

"Let us not become weary in doing good, for at the proper time
we will reap a harvest if we do not give up"
(Galatians 6:9).

Tsunami-ravaged Indonesia

December 26, 2004. A 9.0 magnitude quake under the Indian Ocean created a monstrous tsunami, which instantly devoured the western coast of Indonesia, and claimed four hundred thousand lives. Within thirty-six seconds, at the speed of a jet liner, the tsunami's watery rage annihilated its way inland four kilometers from the beaches. One hundred thousand corpses had to be quickly buried in a mass grave before decomposition and disease set in and millions of people became instantly homeless. The small city of Nias was among the hardest hit, as it was struck by powerful aftershocks, resulting in the additional loss of two thousand lives. Our immediate impulse was to quickly send help, as we felt compelled to reach out to the Indonesian disaster victims, but we were already stretched to full capacity by our ongoing activities in China and North Korea. Nonetheless, we began praying for an avenue with which we could offer assistance in the Indonesian disaster relief efforts.

My wife and I made an impromptu trip to Indonesia to survey the full scope of the devastation, firsthand. Nias had been reduced to a horrific scene of destruction. Its coastline was destroyed and in many towns and villages, concrete stumps were the only remnants left behind of substantial structures, ghostly evidence of a once-thriving city reduced to nothing. A thick stench of rotting death hung grotesquely in the hot, sticky air. Coordinating efforts with volunteers from a local Indonesian church, I arranged for a subsequent visit from a SAM medical team. Upon my return to the U.S, I wasted no time in mobilizing and dispatching that team to Indonesia. Four doctors and one nurse would be treating the injured and aiding in the prevention of virulent epidemic diseases that threatened to cripple the islands further, due to the deadly confluence of insufficient hygiene and intense tropical heat and humidity.

One of the doctors on that Indonesia medical team wrote the following account:

On the day of our arrival, we treated hundreds of injured patients, even skipping lunch to do so. That evening, we barely found a room in an inn, and five of us (four men and one woman) had to share that one room. I believe it was the first time that Mrs. Choi had to share a room with male adults other than her family members! We weren't quite sure that the shoddily built hotel room would hold up should another earthquake happen. However, we were not afraid, as we knew that we were exactly where the Lord would want us to be.

We worked non-stop in sweltering 110 degree heat, full humidity, surviving on very little sleep and instant cups of noodles for sustenance. It was heart wrenching to see the thousands upon thousands injured, and hundreds of thousands of people mourning the loss of their loved ones. I can only pray and hope that our efforts brought a sense of His love and comfort in the midst of this tragedy. May His mercy be upon all those who have suffered.

Indonesia is the world's fifth largest country, with a population of two hundred thirty million people. Indonesia is the largest Muslim nation in the world with 85 percent of the population identifying themselves with the Islam faith. It is also the center of "unreached people" of the world. The Lord has placed a burden in my heart for this region, an expanded vision for world missions beyond China and North Korea. It is my prayer that one day we may have the opportunity to set up SAM clinics there, in conjunction with members of the local Indonesian Christian community.

All in accordance to His plan and His time.

Dear Children, Grow up with Hope

Since 2004 we have supported the Bongsong Orphanage. The orphanage was founded that same year by a young Korean-Chinese woman named Kay Lee, who is its director. At any given time, there are usually ten children living there.

The Bongsong Orphanage is located approximately thirty miles from the Dan Dong Hospital, and, when possible, we send short-term medical mission teams to conduct clinics at the orphanage. I marvel at the vital transformations I have witnessed occurring at the orphanage over the years and, most significantly, in the children. Despondent boys and girls—many of whom have suffered insidious, unspeakably horrible abuses—initially arrive feeling as if they belong nowhere and eventually become gently integrated and securely anchored into a loving family structure. Faces of hollow sadness become adorned with tentative smiles, and the sounds of the slightest hint of laughter and giggles begin to surface. An invalid child, who at one time isolated himself from others, today walks with the assistance of friends and seeks out hugs from anyone within reach. The remarkable transformations seen in these children has made more lucidly evident than ever before the revolutionary and ameliorating power of love. As the children become secure in their warm and loving environment, physical illnesses are healed, wounded hearts are mended, and hurtful memories are replaced with the joy of a lifetime.

No one ever calls them orphans. They do not consider themselves orphans, but instead, part of one big loving family, with the Lord Jesus Christ as their father and head of their family.

One particular evening, Ms. Lee brought a young boy to the Dan Dong Hospital. He was severely wasted and malnourished—so ill that he remained hospitalized under our care for five days. When I asked Ms. Lee the reason for the boy's poor condition, she relayed his tragic story to me:

People in one of the surrounding villages called me for help. They had found the boy on a mountain side, buried alive. He had somehow survived for three days. When I asked who would have done such a horrible thing, they answered, 'We heard that it was the boy's grandfather.'

The boy had been born crippled, and his parents divorced in the midst of poverty and family troubles. The mother took the boy's healthy sister and fled, while the boy remained with his father. But the father wanted nothing to do with his crippled son and left him with his own father, the boy's grandfather. The grandfather apparently wanted nothing to do with the boy either and tried to get rid of him by burying him alive. I cried so hard when I heard this.

Disgust and bilious anger rose within me as I listened to this sickening narrative. "Please pray for him," Ms. Lee pleaded softly. "He still suffers from severe nightmares."

His first night at the Dan Dong Hospital, my colleagues and I gathered around the boy's bed and prayed for him. Each evening thereafter, I would go alone to his hospital room to pray before retiring for the night, "Dear Lord, thank you for protecting and bringing this child to live yet another day according to your special plan for his life. I thank you for bringing this child to us, allowing us to care for him. I trust that you'll heal his deep, deep wounds and strengthen him with your love. I pray that you'll protect him so that no evil spirit can ever touch him again. Please give this child great peace of mind and endless joy of spirit."

Afterward, I would sit silently in his darkened room, listening for a while to the rhythmic sounds of his breathing. Only when I was confident that he was soundly asleep, would I quietly slip out.

Today that little boy is one of those smiling, carefree faces greeting me at the Bongsong Orphanage.

Love conquers all.

Special Vitamins and Minerals for
Pregnant Women and Children

"Severe malnutrition can cause damage to human genes." I was struck by the ominous title of an article appearing in a weekly national U.S. news magazine. The article delved into the dire consequences of malnutrition and starvation as suffered by masses around the globe, living in impoverished and disease-stricken Third World countries. As I read the article, it occurred to me that we should be sending vitamins and special minerals to North Korea.

The consequences of malnutrition can be deleterious and fatal for pregnant women and developing fetuses. Having spent over thirty years as a practitioner and professor of obstetrics and gynecology, no one appreciates more fully than I the blessing and miracle of life that constitutes pregnancy. But this delicate condition can also pose serious health risks. In developed countries, the average mortality rate for pregnant women due to complications is three out of one hundred thousand. In North Korea, that rate is sixty times greater, with the mortality rate being one hundred ten out of one hundred thousand. Many factors contribute to this startling statistic—malnutrition, lack of medical care, poor hygiene—with the single most detrimental and causative factor attributable to malnutrition.

Poor nutrition inhibits proper fetus development, which increases a pregnant woman's risk for miscarriage or even death. Malnutrition during pregnancy also increases the odds of a baby being born with mental retardation and/or other severe life threatening or life impairing conditions. Numerous studies have proven the preventative and protective power of increasing folic acid levels for pregnant women, against many spinal cord and congenital brain deformities in fetuses.

For decades, an underfed North Korean population has slowly withered away from chronic malnutrition. The devastating effects of years of famine are now being observed, most startlingly, in the children. Chronic shortages of food and prolonged starvation has severely stalled and stunted the growth of an entire generation of North Korean children. The most recent nutritional surveys conducted in North Korea by the United Nations produced disturbing findings. Researchers determined that a staggering 62 percent of children under the age of seven suffered from severely stunted growth. And it had been observed that 30 percent of children between the ages of one and two suffered from moderate to severe malnutrition. With development during children's crucial formative years, such as brain development, being progressively impaired due to the lack of food, the physical, psychosocial, and mental capabilities of an entire generation of North Korean children have been irretrievably lost and can never be fully restored or compensated for at a later time.

My SAM colleagues and I came to the unanimous decision to provide North Korea with essential vitamins and special minerals, such as folic acid. We began our "Let's Send Vitamins and Special Minerals to Pregnant Women and Children Campaign."

To jump-start the endeavor, we sent an initial shipment of several tons of fortified vitamins and minerals to North Korea. We also came to the unanimous decision to set up our own vitamin producing factory. The ideal place for such a factory would be either Sin Eu Ju, North Korea, or Pyong Yang, North Korea. However, in either of those cities, we would face hindrances, hurdles, constraints, uncertainty, and no control. As an alternative, we decided to also build a factory near our Dan Dong Hospital. The Chinese government, in a gesture of appreciation for the many contributions we had made in improving the welfare of their people, granted us permission to create a vitamin producing factory that would be 100 percent owned by SAM. In a communist country where the governing ideology is that the people own nothing and the government owns everything, this was truly an example of the Lord's miraculous power paving the way.

Our next step was to obtain the financing. I had every confidence that the Lord would show us the way. He had never failed to provide the means necessary to accomplish His work. As with everything else, we began with prayers on our knees, humbly approaching His throne of grace.

Today in Pyong Yang, North Korea, we have built a factory producing special vitamins and minerals and are currently in the process of building another such manufacturing plant in Dan Dong, China. The goal for each of these facilities is to produce enough supplements to fortify the nutrition of four hundred thousand North Korean pregnant women and children per month. Ten dollars provides enough of these nutrients for one pregnant woman and one child for one month.

One small vitamin. One small gesture of love. One special life. One saved soul.

My Wife's Prayers

After a long, eight-hour flight from New Jersey, it was late in the evening by the time my plane landed at San Francisco International Airport. As I came out of the arrival gate, my wife welcomed me back with a warm hug and a bright smile.

"How did it go?" she asked as we made our way to the car. My wife could be adequately described as "the true power behind the man." As I traveled around the world for speaking engagements, my wife would devote her full time and energy in praying for me. Since the day we were married, she had begun each morning of each day at 4 a.m., rising to pray.

"I'm praying for you, don't worry about anything. Just do your best and follow the Lord's lead." Before I would embark on any speaking engagement, she always encouraged me with those sage words. Upon my return, we would settle into our established routine of each testimonial journey being vicariously shared by her. She would brim with curiosity and excitedly debrief me by asking many detailed questions: "Were the people blessed by what you had to say?"; "What did you share in your sermon?"; "What did you eat?"

Such was the case with my trip to New Jersey: "It was wonderful. I gave four sermons on Sunday, at three different churches. My schedule was so packed that day that I didn't even have time for lunch. Strangely, I didn't feel hungry or tired. I'm thankful because all the pastors responded favorably and promised to pray and support our missions. Pastor Kim told me, 'We had a budget for Chinese missions last year, but, because we didn't find a worthy project to spend it on, we couldn't appropriate it. We're delighted to find a way to help both China and North Korea at the same time through your mission efforts.' On Sunday many people even followed me back to my hotel room to continue our conversations. They didn't want to leave even though I was scheduled to leave early the next morning. The Lord's grace and blessings covered me from start to finish during this entire trip."

She listened intently while driving. When we arrived home, she deftly parked the car in the garage and turned to me, "Okay, this mission has been successfully accomplished. Good job! Now you need to start getting ready for your speaking engagements in Seoul." She grinned as if satisfied with my report.

As I eased out of the car, I asked, "I'm curious, Honey, right after we got married, what was it that you used to pray for so intensely?"

She pondered for a moment. "At first I prayed that you'd be saved and would come to love the Lord and become a person of great faith. Afterward, I prayed that you'd become an evangelist who'd fly all over the world to share the gospel."

"You prayed that for me?" I asked, astonished.

"There was actually a time when I resigned myself to the thought that perhaps it wasn't the Lord's plan for you to become an evangelist because it didn't happen quickly enough. So, I adjusted my prayers and asked the Lord, instead, to allow you to serve as a church deacon and then as an elder, as proof of your good faith. However, the Lord in His amazing grace answered and fulfilled every single one of my prayer requests . . . just not in the order that I presumed it would happen."

As I listened to my wife's startling little testimony, I pronounced, "The Lord answers each and every prayer of truth according to His good timing and will. Keep on praying, Honey. And don't ever stop."

She beamed as brightly as the sun.

I once asked my wife, after seeing the couples we knew renewing their vows on their fortieth wedding anniversary, "Should we also have a fortieth anniversary ceremony next year?"

She mused for a slight moment. "I don't know. Then I'd have to follow you around for another forty years and play background shadow to your missions," she answered while making funny faces.

I laughed.

Without her selfless and dedicated prayers, nurturing care, love, attention, and wisdom, I would be only a sliver of the man I am today. I remain forever indebted to her for her endless devotion and will spend the rest of my life expressing my deepest gratitude and love.

Successful Doctor versus Blessed Doctor

October 2003. My alma mater, Seoul National University Medical School, held its fortieth anniversary for the graduating class of 1963. All one hundred thirty members of our class were asked to vote for the classmate they considered to have the most outstanding career as a physician. Shockingly, my classmates chose me, and at the reunion ceremony I received the award for "The Most Distinguished Seoul National University Medical School Graduate of the Year." I won this award over other candidates I considered much more accomplished and deserving: studied scholars in medicine, renowned medical school professors, and distinguished hospital presidents. In receiving this award, I experienced more joy from my colleagues' kind recognition than any other award I have had the honor to receive. All those years ago, when I had graduated from medical school, I was poor, hungry, and miserable. I was an irascible fellow and terribly misunderstood. Many of my classmates at that time considered me to be an aimless and purposeless student. Forty years later, I could never have fathomed that the Lord would fill my life with such overflowing blessings. Many of my medical school colleagues today have become loyal friends, partners, contributors, and participating members of my mission efforts.

I have a dream.

Someday there will be a high speed train that travels between South Korea and North Korea. There will also be a train traveling between Tokyo and Seoul via a tunnel under the ocean. In my dream we can have breakfast in Tokyo and arrive in Seoul in one hour. One more hour on the train and we will be in Sin Eu Ju, North Korea. We will then cross the Yalu River Bridge to arrive in Dan Dong, China, where we can enjoy a delicious lunch at the Dan Dong Hospital. Afterward we can catch a ride on the train to Beijing, China, where we will then take another train traveling along the Silk Road through Afghanistan, India, and Paris. We will have dinner in Paris, and by the time we arrive in London, it will be time for an evening snack.

I dream that one day the entire world will be traversed like this and that the Dan Dong Hospital will be the central gateway to the West, the 10/40 Window, and all the "unreached" regions of the world. I am filled with excitement at the prospect of missionaries one day being able to ride those trains to take the gospel to the farthest corners of the globe. Missionaries will arise from the most wretched lands and become transformed disciples and devoted apostles of our Lord Jesus Christ. That day is coming. That is the reason that I fly around the world today, as if it were my own backyard.

In a sense, my life has come full circle. For many years I craved success. Intensely. My hardened drive and steely ambition were fueled by an unquenchable need to separate myself from the misery, poverty, and starvation of my youth. With a rushing drive of abandon, I worked astonishingly hard to be better, achieve higher, and acquire more. Acquisitions and accomplishments, success and happiness were all within my control. I was the master of my own future. I determined the course of my own destiny. Did I succeed? I suppose you could say that I did, that I "made it." In a worldly sense, I became a "successful doctor." I had everything I needed and could ask for.

And yet, I was dying inside.

What is the purpose of gaining the world, only to lose your soul in the process? And who is it that the Lord intended for me to be? A blessed doctor. I have walked away from the worldly success I worked so hard to achieve, and I am truly living now. I am alive. I have shed the lingering vestiges of my old life and have returned to the wretched places of the world, the places where I promised myself I would never return, places from which I ran so frantically to escape. And I am filled with inexplicable joy. My medical career was once the modality through which I gained worldly things. My medical career is now the modality through which I fish for souls for the kingdom of heaven. I am a "blessed doctor." The Lord has clothed me in His blessed grace and allowed me to serve Him in this manner. I am humbled.

Until that day of our Lord Jesus' return, poverty will always remain. There will always be loss. There will always be pain. There will always be suffering. But there is also this: until the very last days, He will always be with us. Even as our lives dim and eventually fade away into the dust from whence we came, His love and grace will remain forever.

And in the end, this is what truly matters.

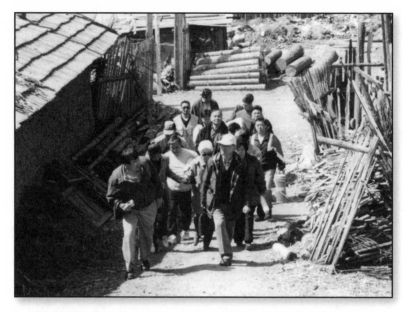

Leading my medical team through a rural village along the Yalu River

Treating patients at Ussrisk, Russia

ACKNOWLEDGMENTS

My deepest thanks go to my family: my wife, Sung Ja, our children and grandchildren, Suzie, Bette, Nathan, Terry, Wui Kyung, Madeleine, Andrew, Angela, and Katelyn. North Korean medical missions was not an endeavor I, alone, undertook. Despite tremendously difficult sacrifices and hardships endured on their part, my family's unwavering and selfless loving support and prayers for North Korean missions made them active participants from the start. I could not have embarked on this work without their steady patience and understanding back home, and am forever indebted to them for their generosity in doing so. They are beautiful and such decent people and I am so proud of each and every one of them.

I am beyond blessed to be surrounded by individuals whom I have the great privilege of calling true friends. Thank you to Attorney Kenneth Ahn and his family for the inspiration to have my 2005 Korean National Best Seller translated into English, which has resulted in this book today. You inspired the idea, nudged it along, and helped to make it a reality. Your enthusiastic support and friendship mean more to me than you will ever know. Thank you to Kimberly Capinpin, Ph.D., for your generous time, effort, valuable insight and contributions in the editing of our manuscript. Thank you to

Pastor John McClendon, for your prayerful and loving heart for North Korea. Thank you to Phyllis Hester and Fred Clark for your unending support and always being there when we need you! You are such important participants in our mission. To Pastor Steven Kim, you are a fearless visionary! Thank you for leading us to the right connections. Thank you to the entire team at Biblica Publishing House: to Volney James for your open hearted mind and courage to publish this book, to John Dunham for your kind support and expert counsel throughout, to Bette Smyth for working with us in getting it right, and to Mike Dworak, for getting us to the right places. Thank you to Douglas Jackson, J.D., Ph.D, for your important partnership and support from the very start. Thank you to Pastor Daniel Kim, for your leadership, prayers, and partnership through Sarang Church. Thank you to Yang Hwa Lee, who is closer than a brother to me. I am indebted to you for your precious tears and loyal heart for our mission. Special thanks to my daughter, Suzie, who spent countless days, sleepless nights, sweat and tears, working on re-edits for this book. Without her efforts, this book simply would not exist. May the Lord inundate your life with the greatest of blessings, dear daughter, for placing such tender value upon your dad's words.

Most importantly, I give all thanks, praise, and honor to our Lord Jesus Christ who has sustained me to this moment. I surrender myself completely to you, Lord, and will spend the rest of my days, as I long as I have breath, thanking you with every fiber of my being, for seeing me as I really am, and choosing to love me, still.